OURS

Also by Sergei Dovlatov

The Compromise
The Zone

OURS

A Russian Family Album

Sergei Dovlatov

Translated from the Russian by
ANNE FRYDMAN

Weidenfeld & Nicolson
New York

This work was supported by a grant from the National Endowment for the Arts.

Published by Weidenfeld & Nicolson, New York
A Division of Wheatland Corporation
841 Broadway
New York, New York 10003-4793

Published in Canada by General Publishing Company, Ltd.

Originally published in Russian as *Nashi* by Ardis Press, Ann Arbor,
Michigan, in 1983

"Uncle Leopold," "Uncle Aron," "Father," "My First Cousin," and "The
Colonel Says I Love You" originally appeared in *The New Yorker*.
"Grandpa Isaak" was first published in *Harper's*; "Aunt Mara" was first
published in *Partisan Review*; "Glasha" was first published in *Grand
Street*.

Library of Congress Cataloging-in-Publication Data

Dovlatov, Sergei.
Ours: a Russian family album.

Translation of: Nashi.
1. Dovlatov, Sergei—Biography—Family.   2. Authors,
Russian—20th century—Biography.   I. Title.
PG3479.6.085Z47613   1989   891.73'44 [B]   88-29990
ISBN 1-55584-281-X

Manufactured in the United States of America
This book is printed on acid-free paper
Designed by Paul Chevannes
First Edition
1   3   5   7   9   10   8   6   4   2

The translator wishes to acknowledge yet again the great help given her by Ms. Rose Raskin and by her husband, Stephen Dixon.

Contents

OURS

Grandpa Isaak

My great-grandfather Moses was a peasant from the village of Sukhovo. The fact is, to be both a Jew and a peasant was rather rare, but it sometimes happened in the Far East.

His son Isaak moved to the city, which is to say, he got things back to normal. At first he lived in Harbin, which is where my father was born. Then he settled on one of the central streets of Vladivostok.

At first my grandfather repaired watches and any kind of household appliance. Then he worked at printing. He was something like a layout man. Then in two years' time he bought his own delicatessen on the city's main boulevard, the Svetlanka.

A wineshop, owned by a certain Zamaraev and bearing the sign "Nectar, Balsam," opened up next door. My grandfather often dropped by to pay the owner a friendly call. The two friends would have a drink together and discuss philosophical matters. Then they would go over to Grandpa's store to have a bite of something tasty. Then they would go back to Zamaraev's. . . .

"You're a man with soul," Zamaraev would say, "even if you are a Jew."

"I'm only a Jew on my father's side," Grandpa would say. "On my mother's side I'm a Dutchman."

"Well, what do you know!" Zamaraev would say approvingly.

In a year's time they had drunk up everything in the wineshop and eaten the delicatessen out of business.

An aged Zamaraev went to live with his sons in Ekaterinograd. As for my grandfather, he went off to war. The Japanese campaign had begun.

During one troop inspection he was noticed by the Tsar himself. Grandpa was almost seven feet tall. He could put an entire apple in his mouth. His mustache drooped to his rifle sling.

The Tsar came up close to Grandpa. Then, with a smile, he poked him in the chest with his finger.

Grandpa was immediately transferred to the Guards. He must have been the only Semite there. He was assigned to an artillery battery. If a horse gave out from exhaustion, Grandpa would drag the cannon through the swamp.

Once, the battery took part in a battle. Grandpa was in the front line of the attack. An armed detachment was supposed to cover the front-line soldiers, but most of the guns were silent. My grandfather's back, it turned out, was blocking their view of the enemy.

4

Grandpa returned home from the front with a .375-caliber rifle and a few medals. It seems he even got a Georgevsky Cross.

He lived it up for a week. Then he took a job as maître d' in the Edem eating establishment. Once, he quarreled with an incompetent waiter. He began to roar, banged his fist on a table. The fist ended up in a desk drawer.

Grandpa did not like disorder. For that reason, he held a negative view of the Revolution. More than that, he even slowed its progress a little. It happened like this:

At the outbreak of the Revolution, masses of people from the outskirts of town began rushing toward the center of the city. Grandpa decided it was a pogrom against the Jews. He got out his rifle and went up to the roof. When the crowds drew near, he began firing into the air. He was the only inhabitant of Vladivostok to oppose the Revolution. Nevertheless, the Revolution won. The great mass of people made it to the center of town by the alleyways.

After the Revolution, Grandpa settled down. He became a modest craftsman once again. There were still times, though, when he drew attention to himself. In one such instance, he damaged the reputation of an American firm called Merkher, Merkher and Co.

This American firm was exporting collapsible beds to the Far East by way of Japan, though they were only called "collapsible beds" much later. At the time, they were a sensational novelty, sold under the name the Magic Bed. The beds looked about the same as they do now: colorful sailcloth, mattress, springs, aluminum frame.

My progressive grandfather made his way to the trade center. A bed had been set up on a special raised platform.

"We will now demonstrate this novelty for you!" the salesman cried. "The bachelor's dream! Indispensable for travel! Comfort and luxury! Does anyone wish to try it out?"

"I wish," my grandfather said. He pulled off his boots without unlacing them and lay down.

There was a loud crack and the springs sang out. Grandpa found himself on the floor.

With an unperturbed smile, the salesman opened another floor sample. The same sounds occurred. Grandpa cursed under his breath and rubbed his back.

The salesman opened a third collapsible bed.

This time the springs held. The aluminum legs, however, gave way in silence. Grandpa made a soft landing.

Soon the hall was littered with the wreckage of wonder beds. Tatters of colorful canvas drooped on the floor, twisted frames gleamed dimly.

After some haggling, Grandpa bought a sandwich and went home.

The reputation of the American firm was severely damaged. Merkher, Merkher and Co. began trading in crystal chandeliers.

Grandpa Isaak ate a great deal. He sliced thick loaves of bread not crosswise but lengthwise. When he and Grandma Raya were invited out to dinner, Grandma was always blushing on account of him. Before leaving the house, Grandpa was fed a full meal. This did not help. He ate pieces of bread folded in half. He drank vodka out of cream-soda glasses. When the hostess was clearing the table for dessert, he would ask her to leave the aspics. On arriving back home, he would sit down for supper with a sigh of relief. . . .

Grandpa had three sons. The youngest, Leopold, went off

6

to China when he was just a young man. From there he went to Belgium.

The two older sons, Mikhail and Donat, were inclined toward the arts. They left provincial Vladivostok behind them and settled in Leningrad. Grandpa and Grandma soon followed after them.

The sons married. Compared with their father, the sons seemed puny and helpless. Both daughters-in-law were rather taken with Grandpa.

He got himself a job working as a kind of manager for a housing office. Evenings he repaired watches and hot plates. He was still as strong as ever.

It happened once in Shcherbakov Lane that a truckdriver insulted him, probably calling him something like "kike face." Grandpa grabbed the side of the moving truck and stopped it. He pushed aside the driver, who had jumped out of the cab. Then he lifted the truck by its bumper and turned it on its side, crosswise, in the middle of the road.

The headlights of the truck rested against a bathhouse. The back end lay in the flower beds of Shcherbakov Square.

Once he realized what had happened, the driver began to weep. He alternately cried and threatened.

"I'll jack it back up!" he said.

"Go ahead and try," Grandpa told him.

The truck blocked the lane for two days. Then a derrick was called in to remove it.

"Why didn't you just punch him in the jaw?" my father asked.

Grandpa thought about this and said, "I was afraid I'd get carried away."

As I've already said, his youngest son, Leopold, had settled in Belgium. Once, a man he knew there came to see the family while visiting the USSR. He was called Monya. Monya brought Grandpa a tuxedo and a huge inflatable giraffe. The giraffe, it turned out, was really a hat rack.

Monya railed against capitalism, was enthusiastic about socialist industry, then went home. Soon afterward, Grandpa was arrested and charged with being a Belgian spy. He was given ten years "without correspondence privileges." What this really meant was that he was shot. Anyway, he would never have survived ten years in a prison camp. Hunger is hard for a healthy man to endure, arbitrary rules and brutality even more so. . . .

More than twenty years later, my father, after much effort, had Grandpa's name rehabilitated "for lack of corpus delicti."

For me the questions are: Just what was going on back then? In the name of what, exactly, was that daft and amusing life cut short?

I often think of my grandfather, though I never knew him. For instance, if one of my friends says in surprise, "How can you drink rum out of a teacup?" I immediately think of Grandpa.

Or my wife may say to me, "Tonight we're going to the Dombrovskys for supper. We should get you something to eat beforehand." Again he comes to mind.

He also came to mind when I was in a prison cell. . . .

I have a few photographs of Grandpa. When my grandchildren leaf through the family album, it won't be hard for them to mistake us for one another.

8

Grandfather
Stepan

My grandfather on my mother's side was known for his harsh temperament. Even for a native of the Caucasus he was considered unusually irascible. His wife and children trembled at his glance.

It seems to me that his oppressive nature was the result of his upbringing. When he was a child, his peasant father used to beat him with firewood logs. Once, his father even lowered him into an abandoned well in a bucket, and kept him down there like that for about two hours. Then he lowered a piece of cheese and a half bottle of Napareuli wine in another bucket. Then Grandpa's father let a whole hour go by before he hauled him up out of the well, wet and drunk. . . .

Maybe that was why Grandpa grew up to be so stern and irritable.

He was tall, elegant, and proud. He worked as a salesman in Epstein's clothing store, and in his declining years was a co-owner.

He was remarkably handsome. Across the street from his house lived numerous members of Prince Chikvaidze's family. When Grandpa crossed the street, the young Chikvaidze girls—Eteri, Nana, and Galatea—would peek out the window to watch him.

His entire family obeyed him unquestioningly. As for him, he bowed to no one. This included higher forces. One of my grandfather's duels with God ended in a draw.

It had been predicted that an earthquake would hit Tiflis, as the city of Tbilisi was then called. Meteorological centers already existed, and besides, there were omens from folklore and signs of nature that people could recognize for themselves. Priests rushed from house to house to warn everyone.

The inhabitants of Tiflis left their apartments, taking their valuables with them. Many left the city for good. Those who remained made campfires in the public squares.

Thieves calmly went about plundering the wealthier neighborhoods. They carried off furniture, dishes, and firewood.

There was only one house in Tiflis in which a bright light burned. To be precise, only one room of that house: my grandfather's study. He did not wish to abandon his home. All his relatives had tried to convince him otherwise. "You will perish, Stepan!" they had said.

Grandpa frowned with displeasure, then gloomily and solemnly uttered the word, "*Ka-a-kem!*" (which translates—please excuse this—as "I crap on you!").

Grandma took the children to a vacant lot. They carried

out of the house everything they absolutely needed, took the dog and the parrot.

The earthquake began at the break of day. The very first tremor destroyed the city water supply. Within ten minutes, hundreds of buildings collapsed. Spear-shaped clouds of dust hung above the city, rosy with sunlight. Finally the tremors ceased. Grandma and the children rushed home to Olginskaya Street.

The street was piled with smoking debris. All around, women were sobbing, dogs were howling. Jackdaws were making eerie circles in the pale morning sky.

Our house had ceased to be. In its place, Grandma saw a pile of bricks and boards covered with dust.

In the center of the ruin sat my grandfather, in a deep armchair. He had dozed off. A newspaper lay on his knees. A bottle of wine stood by his leg.

"Stepan!" Grandma screamed. "God has punished us for our sins! He has destroyed our home!"

Grandfather opened his eyes, looked at his watch, then slapped his palms together and commanded, "Breakfast!"

"The Lord has left us without a roof!" Grandma lamented.

"Eh-eh," my grandfather said. Then he counted the children.

"What will become of us, Stepan? Who will shelter us?"

Grandpa got angry. "The Lord deprived us of a roof," he said. "You deprive us of breakfast. . . . And the one who will shelter us is Beglar Fomich. I stood godfather to two of his sons. The older one turned out to be a bandit. . . . Beglar Fomich is a good man. It's just a pity he waters his wine. . . ."

"The Lord is merciful," Grandma said softly.

Grandpa frowned. His eyebrows drew together. Then he spoke in a clipped, didactic way. "That is not so. It is Beglar who will have mercy. A pity he waters the Napareuli."

"The Lord will punish you again, Stepan!" Grandma said, frightened.

"*Ka-a-kem!*" Grandpa answered. . . .

In his old age, his character became completely impossible. Relatives stopped inviting him to visit; he insulted everyone. He was even rude to those older than he—a phenomenon most rare in the East.

One look from him and women dropped dishes.

In his last years, Grandpa no longer even got up. He sat in a deep armchair on the porch. If someone passed by the house, he would shout, "Get out of here, you thief!" while he gripped the bronze head of his heavy walking stick, which he always kept within reach. A danger zone formed around Grandpa about a yard and a half in radius. That was the length of his stick.

I have often tried to understand why my grandfather was so morose. What made him such a misanthrope? He was well-to-do, possessed a commanding appearance and a superb constitution. He had four children and a faithful, loving wife.

Perhaps the universe, such as it was, did not suit him. I wonder, did it not suit him in its entirety, or just in certain details? Was it the changing of the seasons? The indestructible order of life and death? The law of gravity? The contradiction of sea and dry land? I don't know.

My grandfather died a terrible death. His second duel with God ended tragically.

For ten years he sat in the armchair. In the end, he no longer held on to his walking stick; he just frowned.

(Oh, if looks could serve as technological weapons!)

He became a feature of the landscape, a significant and arresting detail of the local architecture. It was said that jackdaws sometimes landed on his shoulder.

At the end of our street, beyond the market, was a deep ravine. At the bottom of it, a stream foamed and wound between gray, gloomy boulders. If you looked far down the shore, you could see the white bones of dead horses, or pieces of wrecked wooden carts lying strewn about.

Children were not permitted to play near there. Wives would say to their drunken husbands returning at dawn, "Thank God! I thought you had fallen into the ravine."

One day, on a summer morning, my grandfather suddenly stood up. Stood up and left the house with a strong step.

As he crossed the street, Eteri, Nana, and Galatea Chikvaidze, long since married and overweight, watched him from behind their windows.

Tall and straight, he headed toward the market. If anyone greeted him, he did not respond.

At home his disappearance was not noticed right away, just as you might not immediately notice the absence of a poplar, a rock, or a stream.

Grandfather stood on the edge of the ravine. He threw away his walking stick. Raised his hands. Then stepped forward.

He ceased to be there.

A few minutes later, Grandma came running, followed by the neighbors. They screamed and wept loudly. Only toward evening did the sobbing die down.

And only then, through the unceasing noise of the stream skirting the gloomy boulders, could they hear, contemptuous and menacing: *"Ka-a-kem!"*

Uncle Roman

Uncle Roman Stepanovich loved to say, "If you're healthy in body, likewise in mind!" In his youth he had been a Tbilisi *kinto*. It's a difficult word to translate. A *kinto* is not a rowdy, nor a drunkard, nor a "social parasite," though he gets into brawls, gets drunk, and doesn't work. Maybe "hell-raiser" would be the right word. It's hard to say.

My uncle owned a huge dagger. From early on, he adored Napareuli wine and fleshy blondes. The chief quality of a real *kinto*, though, is his wit, and my uncle's sense of humor was distinctly his own. To give an example, this is how my then fourteen-year-old uncle managed to darken the jubilee celebration of the Georgian Soviet Socialist Republic:

The seventh year of the republic, a significant anniversary, was being widely observed in Tbilisi. When the day arrived, people filled the Leibknecht Palace of Culture to capacity. High-ranking administrators delivered speeches. After them came representatives of the city's ethnic minorities. My aunt, Uncle's sister, had been chosen to speak for the Armenian community. Her name was Aniela, and she had spent two weeks rehearsing her speech.

"It has already been seven years," she began.

The hall grew quiet. "It has already been seven years," Aunt Aniela repeated.

Somewhere, someone was tapping a metal coat-check tag on an armrest. Someone else was making his way on tiptoe up the aisle.

"It has already been seven years," young Aunt Aniela said, her voice growing stronger. Behind her back, the Generalissimo squinted slyly from his portrait. Complete silence fell. And then, through the hall, my uncle's voice rang out:

"It's already been seven years and no one's married Aniela!"

Aunt Aniela ran sobbing off the stage. Uncle Roman was held at the police station for twenty-four hours. . . .

Sometime before the Second World War, my uncle decided to apply to the university to study philosophy, a natural decision for a young man who had no concrete goal as yet. People whose orientation in life is vague and cloudy are often the ones who dream of studying philosophy.

Uncle completed the written part of the application, but he also had to pass an oral exam in Russian literature. On the day of the exam, he stopped each person coming out of the examination room and asked, "Excuse me, my friend! What was the question they gave you?"

"Pushkin," the first person said.

"Wonderful!" my uncle exclaimed. "Just what I forgot to study."

"Tolstoy," the second person said.

"Wonderful!" Uncle said. "Just what I forgot to study."

"Gogol," the third person said.

"Wonderful!" Uncle said. "Just what I forgot to study."

Finally his turn came, and the examiners called him in. He stepped up to the table, pulled a ticket out of a box and read his assigned theme: "Dostoyevski's literary career."

"*Vai!* Woe is me!" my uncle cried. "Just what I forgot to study."

My uncle was happy when the war began. People like him are valued in wartime. Even in peacetime he loved to raise hell.

He returned a lieutenant colonel. War had made a man of him.

Like all discharged lieutenant colonels, he was put in charge of security technology at his place of work, the Light-beam factory. (Full colonels are assigned to head personnel departments.) It's possible that he knew something about security technology, or at least it shouldn't be ruled out. What all his energy went into, though, was planning mass athletic events. Uncle organized swimming competitions, established cross-country skiing meets, supervised volleyball matches. He was often written about in the newspapers.

At the age of sixty-three, my uncle was an excellent skier and could still win fistfights. "If you're healthy in body, likewise in mind," he was always saying.

For me, Uncle Roman felt sincere contempt. I didn't do morning exercises. Didn't douse myself with icy water. And generally hated sudden exertions. If insulted, I tended to back down.

I was insulted very rarely, by the way, maybe three times in my entire life. All three times were by my uncle. "Intellectual!" he would shout. "Old woman! Sickly civilian!"

If asked who his favorite author was, he would quickly answer, "Martin Eden."

He could spend hours talking about his prowess in fighting, and he embellished a good deal in the telling. Whenever I asked him about the war, though, he was stubbornly silent. He didn't like to talk about it. I don't know why.

He had children by Anna Grigorevna Sukharova, a boy and a girl. My uncle visited them regularly. He inspected their composition books, signed their report cards, and invariably instructed them, "If you're healthy in body, likewise in mind!"

On one of his visits, Anna Grigorevna was busy preparing something in the kitchen while he was playing with the children. Suddenly he broke wind. The children started laughing. Anna Grigorevna went to see what was happening, stood in the doorway with folded arms, and said solemnly, "Whatever people say, children need their father! See how happily they play, joke, and laugh with him."

Uncle Roman also had a wife, Galina Pavlovna, who worked as a "medical person," as she called herself. Uncle loved and respected her, since she shared his philosophic credo, "If you're healthy in body, likewise in mind."

Once, while my uncle was away at work, the doorbell of their apartment rang. Galina had just come home to have lunch. She went to the door and asked, "Who's there?"

A male voice answered, "Give my pregnant wife a drink of water."

Galina opened the door, and a large man walked into the foyer. He pulled out a sharpened rasp and without saying a word stabbed Galina in the belly. She rushed to the telephone and managed to call my uncle, losing consciousness as she screamed, "Roma! Save me! I'm being murdered!"

My uncle arrived thirty minutes later by truck. Galina, meanwhile, had been taken to the hospital in an ambulance. The attacker had been surrounded and seized by the neighbors. When they were tying his hands behind his back, he had burst out laughing. No one could ever discover a motive for what he had done. He must have been deranged, and that explained it.

My uncle wept that entire evening. And when Galina came home from the hospital, he bought a German shepherd.

They called her Golda. This choice of name bespoke my uncle's sense of humor, as well as a slight streak of anti-Semitism. Many Armenians, especially Georgian Armenians, did not like Jews, although it would have been more logical for them to dislike Russians, Georgians, or Turks. Jews, for their part, did not feel much warmth toward Armenians. Apparently, people at the bottom of the social ladder don't much care for others like them. They prefer to love the masters, or, if worse comes to worst, themselves.

So the German shepherd was called Golda. At first she was a charming, pigeon-toed puppy. Then she grew up and started being shown in dog shows. Once, she even won second prize for something. Then one day, she attacked Galina for no reason and bit her badly. Uncle wanted to shoot the dog, but his wife talked him out of it. Golda was given away to a kennel.

Uncle Roman kept doing morning exercises, was tight-muscled and trim. He could jump onto a moving tram and bring any ruffian to reason. Only he rarely encountered ruffians, and there were fewer and fewer trams in the city. . . .

And then suddenly I was told that my uncle was in a psychiatric hospital. Galina Pavlovna said it was a "neural clinic," but it was actually a psychiatric hospital.

I went out to see him there. The hospital was made up of a few standard brick buildings surrounded by scraggly bushes and trees. Patients wearing identical gray hospital gowns were walking along the paths. The gowns were either too big or too small, as if all the tall people had intentionally been given small sizes, and all those of frail build had been given enormous ones.

Most of the patients walked by themselves. A few gesticulated in a restrained, otherworldly way. I found I wasn't frightened, only sorry for them.

Finally my uncle was escorted out. To my surprise, he looked animated and quite hale and hearty. He even had a bit of a tan. He said the food was fine, and the best thing about the place was that he could spend so much time outdoors.

Then Uncle drew close to me, looked around anxiously, and said in a whisper, "Listen to me carefully. The four-eyes here have cooked up a mammoth conspiracy."

"Who?" I asked, not understanding. Uncle did not answer. Instead, forcing a smile, a façade of great gaiety, he said, "This is going to be much worse than St. Bartholomew's eve."

I got completely flustered. I hadn't been prepared for this. I didn't know how to act, whether to argue or just go along with him.

A young attendant walked past, carrying a drinking urn. Near the spigot was an inscription in dark letters: WATER.

My uncle whistled nonchalantly. The boy disappeared behind the trees.

"There's going to be blood!" my uncle said, shaking his head.

Out of a feeling of horror, I started playing a strange role. "Maybe everything will still turn out all right?"

"Expect no mercy," my uncle said quietly. "Some will be wiped out, others will be forced to join. . . . But I have a plan. Listen to me carefully."

Uncle again leaned over, and, winking slyly, he said, "Even the most brilliant plan is vulnerable. A chain is only as strong as its weakest link. The slightest movement and the cards fall. . . . The rules of the game, as they are called, have been eliminated. The trick is to make an absolutely unforeseen move. And I've discovered it. Listen carefully."

Uncle stopped smiling and began to speak like an officer, abrupt and laconic. "The first move is the crucial one. The second is for insurance, in case of failure. Don't take notes," he said, interrupting himself.

"Good," I said.

"And remember. First of all, smoke unfiltered cigarettes, and only unfiltered. Second, always wear two pairs of underpants."

Uncle laughed triumphantly and rubbed his hands together. "Did you understand?" he said.

"Yes," I said.

"The plan will remain a secret. Not a word to anyone, not even those closest to you. Otherwise all is lost. Await my further instructions. And now it's time for me to go. Be well. Thank you for the fruit. Though it too is merely a figment of pure water."

And he walked away, in the absurd gown, with a light, sporty gait.

A month later he was well. We saw each other at family occasions. Uncle would chuckle shyly.

He would talk about jogging the whole way around the Forestry Institute each day. About how he felt healthier and fitter than ever before.

Grated vegetables would be prepared especially for him. Galina Pavlovna would sit next to him, the scars of the dog bites dark on her arms.

I imagined my uncle jogging early in the morning by the fence of the Forestry Institute.

Whither, O Lord?

Uncle Leopold

The life of my uncle Leopold was enveloped in an exotic mist. His fate excited my imagination for many long years, though that's all over now.

My Jewish grandfather in Vladivostok had three sons, just as in a fairy tale. The oldest, Mikhail, grew up withdrawn and unsocial. He wrote poetry. He managed to put together a group of Futurists there in the Far East provinces. Maya-kovski himself sent him a letter, one only moderately rude and more friendly than his usual. My father still has two of the books his elder brother wrote. The first is entitled *Moo-oooo*. The other title I forget, but it has a complicated algebraic formula in it. The poems are quite silly. One love poem ends like this:

> I was all atremble, and I yearned
> To beat my brow against a wall, to fall . . .

I remember a nasty remark about these lines in Mayakovski's review of the work, which my father saved: "A fool prays to God and ends up cracking his skull."

Mikhail was such a reclusive person that his relatives had no idea of his interests. Once, when my father, Donat, was a young actor, he ran into him backstage at the Bryansk Summer Theater. Both brothers, it turned out, were part of the same touring theatrical revue. Mikhail was giving dramatic readings, and Donat was singing satirical songs.

So the two older brothers were drawn to art and literature. The youngest, Leopold, took a different route, a more practical one. He grew up a hustler.

At fourteen he was speculating in tobacco around the port. He bought cigars from foreign sailors and sold them in the evening at the Zimmerman brothers' restaurant. Then he moved on to stockings and cosmetics. If asked, he would escort foreigners to the brothel on Kosaya Street. Along with all this, he boxed at the Icarus Athletic Club and played the trumpet in the public gardens on Sundays. Before his eighteenth birthday, he had brought off his first genuine scam. It happened like this:

One day, a melancholy, modest youth entered one of the major stores of the city. Under his arm was a violin wrapped in crumpled newspaper. He went over to the proprietor, whose name, I think, was Tanakis, and said, "It's pouring outside, and I'm worried my violin will get wet. Could I leave it here for a little while?"

"Why not?" Tanakis answered indifferently.

An hour later, a well-dressed foreigner with an enormous, suspiciously red mustache appeared in the store. For a long time he looked over the imported goods set out on the shelves. Then he lifted some crumpled newspaper and exclaimed, "It can't be! I don't believe it! Tell me I'm dreaming! What a stroke of luck—a genuine Stradivarius! I'll buy it from you."

"It's not for sale," Tanakis said.

"But I'll pay any amount you want!"

"I'm very sorry—"

"Fifteen thousand in cash!"

"I truly regret this, monsieur—"

"Twenty!" the foreigner shouted.

Tanakis blushed slightly. "I will speak to the fellow who owns it."

"To you I will give a generous commission. After all, this is a genuine Stradivarius! Oh, please don't forget, don't forget me!" And he left.

A while later, the pale youth returned. "I've come for my violin," he said.

"Sell it to me," Tanakis said.

"I cannot," the youth answered sadly. "Alas, I cannot. It was a gift from my grandfather. It's the one valuable thing I own."

"I'll pay you two thousand in cash."

The young man was close to tears. "As it happens, I am in pressing need of funds. The money you offer would be extremely welcome. I would be able to go to a health resort, as Dr. Shvarts has recommended. But still, I cannot do it. It was a present—"

"Three," the store owner said.

"Alas, I cannot."

"Five!" Tanakis roared. Meantime, he must have been figuring to himself, I give this kid five, the foreigner pays me twenty plus commission, that comes to . . .

"Grandfather, forgive me," the young man whimpered. "Forgive me and don't be angry. Circumstances force me to take this step!"

Tanakis was already counting out the bills. The youth kissed the violin. Then, close to sobbing, he left. Tanakis rubbed his hands in satisfaction.

The young man turned the corner and stopped, carefully counted the money, took the enormous red mustache out of his pocket and threw it in a ditch. Then he marched off. . . .

A few months later, Leopold ran away from Vladivostok. He got to China in the hold of an ocean liner, where a rat bit him. From China he headed for Europe, and he settled for some reason in Belgium.

Stern as ever, Grandpa Isaak refused to read his postcards. "A no-goodnik," Grandpa said. "A blot on the family name." And he seemed to forget Leopold's existence.

Grandma wept and prayed in secret. "In that Belgium of his, there are probably nothing but goyim," she kept saying.

A few years went by. The dark times of Stalin's rule began. Mail from Leopold stopped getting through.

Then a fellow named Monya arrived from the West. He brought news of Leopold and stayed with Grandpa and Grandma for a week. He said Leopold had gone into business for himself. Monya was enthusiastic about the sweep of Stalin's Five-Year Plan. He liked to sing the inspirational song "Fly forward, our locomotive!" At the same time, he was plainly ill-bred. He would roar from the toilet, so that the whole apartment could hear, "Paper! Paper!" And Grandma would slip a newspaper under the door.

Then Monya left Russia, very pleased with his visit. A few months later, Grandpa was arrested, accused of spying for Belgium, and shot.

Specific grounds for this charge were not cited. It was enough to have relatives living abroad. Though maybe it mattered that Grandpa was not sufficiently enthusiastic about the sweep of Stalin's Five-Year Plan. Then, too, he was a little too noticeable—tall, angry, and loud voiced. Under dictators, people who stand out do not fare well.

For a long time, the youngest brother went largely unmentioned, and even less so when Donat and Mikhail moved from Vladivostok to Leningrad. My father became a stage director there.

Leningrad was also the destination of a young aspiring actress from Georgia. That was how my parents met and how everything conspired, as they say, to bring about my birth.

In the next few years, a great deal happened: war, victory, yet another flare-up of terror. Mikhail had died of tuberculosis during the siege of Leningrad; Grandma died after the war. My parents divorced. Leopold's existence was barely remembered.

And then the comparatively liberal Khrushchev years began. Leopold's name started to turn up in my father's conversation—was he still alive? still in Europe?—and for me his escapades took their place among the adventures of James Fenimore Cooper and Mayne Reid heroes. One day in 1961, my father happened to be passing the central telegraph office in Leningrad. He stopped in to chat with a friend who was a clerk there. From her he learned that the office housed a complete set of telephone books of the capitals of Europe. My father asked for the Brussels telephone book, and immediately found his own rather uncommon last name.

"Could I actually make a call to Brussels?" he asked.

"Why not?"

Within three minutes, they had the Brussels number for him. A familiar voice said distinctly, "Hello!"

"Leopold!" my father screamed.

"Hold on, Dodik," Leopold said. "I'll shut off the TV."

The brothers began to correspond. Leopold wrote that he had a wife named Helene, a son named Philippe, a daughter named Edith, and a poodle called Igor. He had his own business. He sold lumber and building materials. Lumber was getting more expensive, which suited him fine. Inflation had nevertheless nearly ruined him. Leopold described his poverty in this manner: "All my houses need repairs. The parking lot hasn't been repaved in four years."

My father's letters sounded a bit sunnier: "I am a writer and theater director. I live in a small, cozy apartment." (He referred here to his tiny room, partitioned off with plywood.) "My wife has just been driving through the Baltic republics." (Actually, my father's second wife did sometimes take a union bus to Riga to buy stockings.) "And, as for inflation, I have no idea what it is."

My father besieged Leopold with mementos of Russia. He sent him a whole flotilla of wooden spoons and bowls, a cupronickel replica of Leo Tolstoy's samovar, several figurines in semiprecious Ural stone, and a jubilee edition of Maeterlinck the size of a headstone.

Leopold responded with a snowy linen handkerchief in a

beautiful package. Then he sent my father a nylon-tricot pullover bearing the words EDDIE SHAPIRO—WHEELS AND TIRES.

My father was not to be outdone. He called up a friend who was a city official, and with his help managed to obtain a one-of-a-kind souvenir: a huge block of sugar weighing about four kilos and shaped like an artillery piece. It bore the inscription, in old lettering, TRADING HOUSE OF FIRST GUILD MERCHANT ELPIDIFOR FOMIN.

It was an exact copy of a pre-Revolutionary sugar carving. Such objects were very much in vogue in the Khrushchev years. The intelligentsia would decorate their apartments with antiques, which were difficult to obtain. They were sold only in special stores closed to everyone but members of the high-ranking elite.

My father's connection had to be thanked with cognac. The one-of-a-kind souvenir was sent off to Leopold.

Two months later, my father was notified that a package from abroad had arrived for him. It weighed ten-and-a-half kilos and had a charge of sixty-eight rubles due on it.

My father became terrifically excited. On the way to the post office, he kept fantasizing aloud, "A tape recorder . . . a sheepskin coat . . . whiskey . . ." He asked me, "How much do you think a sheepskin coat weighs?"

"About three kilos," I said.

"So he must have sent three sheepskin coats."

The clerk at the central post office brought out a heavy box. "We'll take a taxi back," my father said.

Finally we reached home. Laughing nervously, my father got out a chisel and pried off the plywood top, which came away with a squeal.

"That idiot!" my father groaned. Inside the box were ten

kilos of yellowish granulated sugar. My father raged on. "That no-goodnik! Thinks we're savages! I send him an amazing object and he figures we don't have granulated sugar!"

About eight years later, the time of emigration began. The Soviet intelligentsia headed for the West. This included our own loony family, and with good reason, since by that time I had become a "suppressed" writer and had even spent some time in jail.

My wife and daughter were the first to leave. They stayed in Rome for a while and then moved on to America. Then my mother and I managed to get exit visas. My father was still hesitating. I took Leopold's address with me when I left.

My mother and I waited in Austria for permission to enter the States. Reinhardt, the owner of the Admiral Hotel in Vienna, was very kind to us. Every morning we were served tea with warm rolls and jam. Every morning Reinhardt would invariably ask, "Would you like a shot of vodka?" He also lent us a radio and an electric toaster.

Sometimes Reinhardt and I would sit and talk in the evening. I learned that he had come from East Germany, that he was a construction engineer by training, that the hotel business was not much to his liking, though it brought in a good deal of money.

"Are you married?" I asked.

"Erika lives in Salzburg."

"They say that marriages on the brink of divorce are the ones that last the longest."

"We've gone beyond the brink, but somehow we're still married. Does that surprise you?"

"No," I said.

"Did you ever belong to the Party?"

"No. In my opinion, the Party should consist of one person."

"That's the truth. What about the Young Communist League?"

"Yes. That happens automatically."

"I understand. How do you like the West?"

"After prison I like everything."

"My father was arrested in 1940. He called Hitler '*das braunes Schwein.*' "

"Was he a Communist?"

"No. He wasn't a Commie. He wasn't even red. He just stood out. He was an educated man. He knew Latin. Do you know Latin?"

"No."

"Neither do I. And my children won't know it, either, which is a pity. I suspect that Latin and Rod Stewart don't go together."

"Who is Rod Stewart?"

"A madman with a guitar. Would you like a glass of vodka?"

"I would."

"I'll bring some sandwiches."

"Not essential."

"You're right."

I had written to Uncle Leopold soon after we arrived. He called the hotel and announced that he would fly to Vienna at the end of the week. He would be staying at the Coliseum Hotel, he said, and asked me not to eat breakfast on Saturday. "I'm taking you out to a good restaurant," he said.

Saturday morning, I sat in the Coliseum lobby. This hotel was a sight more elegant than ours. Rare breeds of dog were being walked through the lobby. The man checking coats looked like a movie star.

At exactly eleven, my uncle came downstairs. I recognized him at once. Leopold looked much like my father—tall, elegant, with a beautiful set of false teeth. Beside him walked a youthful-looking woman.

I knew that I ought to embrace this man, who was, in actuality, a complete stranger. We embraced. I kissed Helene's hand, in which she held an umbrella.

"Are you huge!" Leopold shouted. "And where's Mama?"

"She wasn't feeling too well."

"What a pity! I saw her photograph. You look very much like her."

I handed him a package. In it was caviar, wooden *matreshki* dolls, and a linen tablecloth.

"Thank you! We'll leave this with the porter. I have some presents for you, too, but now we'll go to the restaurant. Do you like restaurants?"

"I never really thought about it."

"This place has nice music, beautiful women. . . . What do you plan to do in America?"

"I don't really know."

"Do you have any sort of profession?"

"Mainly I'm a writer. I write."

"In English?"

"Unfortunately, no."

"That kind of work doesn't pay very well."

"That's not important."

"Don't be so sure."

"As I see it, money is not the main thing."

We walked toward the center of town. Leopold talked nonstop. Helene smiled in silence.

"Look at all these cars! Have you ever seen foreign cars before?"

"Yes. Leningrad was full of tourists."

"Do you want to get a car?"

"They say you have to have one in America."

"Vienna is a small city. So is Brussels, for that matter. There are much bigger cars in America. And what stores they have there! Are there department stores in Leningrad?"

"There are some," I said.

"I heard you were having a big economic crisis there."

"I hadn't noticed. We're probably just used to them."

"So then why did you leave?"

"At the moment," I said, "it's the thing to do."

"You're so enormous! I bet the women like you?"

"That remains to be seen."

"I understand. Your wife is already in America. We saw her in Rome. She had some plastic thing instead of a handbag. I bought her a good leather purse for sixty dollars. Hold it, everyone! This is where we'll eat. I've always found this a fine restaurant."

We went inside, took off our coats, and sat down at a table by the window. A little band was playing the usual restaurant music, not too loudly. Beautiful women, somehow, were nowhere in sight.

"Order anything you want," Leopold said. "Maybe you'd like a steak, or some game?"

"Anything at all. Whatever you choose."

"Some delicacies, perhaps? Do you like delicacies?"

"I don't know."

"How can that be?" Leopold exclaimed.

"Anything will be fine."

My uncle got slightly offended. "You have to take these things seriously." Then he added, "I love delicacies, but I've got a sick liver. I'll order you a salmon pâté and some asparagus."

"Excellent."

"And what will you drink?"

"Something strong. Would vodka be all right?"

"It's too early. I think either white wine or tea."

"Tea," I said.

"And pistachio ice cream."

"Fine."

"What would you like to drink?" Leopold asked his wife.

"Vodka," Helene said.

"What?" Leopold asked her again.

"Vodka, vodka, vodka!" she said.

A waiter came to our table. He was dark haired and stocky, probably Yugoslavian or Hungarian.

"This is my nephew from Russia," Leopold said.

He disappeared, and the music suddenly stopped. There was a light riffling sound of sheet music. Then I heard the opening bars of "Moscow Nights."

The waiter reappeared. His face was now glowing and shiny.

"Thank you," I said.

"He'll get a good tip," Leopold whispered to me. The waiter took our order, smiling mysteriously, like a trusted accomplice helping with a difficult, risky undertaking.

"Oh, yes, I almost forgot," Leopold exclaimed. "Can you

tell me how my parents died? I kept asking your father in my letters, but he never did say."

"Grandma Raya died in 1946 of heart failure. I remember her a little."

"And your grandpa?"

"I never knew him. He was arrested before the war."

"Arrested? For what?"

"Just arrested. In those days it happened all the time."

"Was he against the Communists?"

"I don't think so."

"So what did he do? What reason did they give?"

"Huge numbers of people were arrested during that time. It had nothing to do with reason."

"God, what a savage place," Leopold said in a muffled voice. "Explain it to me."

"I'm afraid I couldn't. Dozens of books have been written about it."

Leopold wiped his eyes with a handkerchief. "I can't read books. I work too hard. . . . So then he died in prison?"

I didn't feel like telling him that Grandpa had been shot. Even mentioning the arrest led nowhere good. I'd seem to be saying Leopold was indirectly to blame. Some might argue he was; but anyway, how could he understand?

"He died in prison?"

I nodded.

"What an awful country! I've been to America, to Israel. I've been everywhere in Europe, but I would never go to Russia. It's good for chess and for ballet, but that's it. That and police action. Do you like chess?"

"I like to play. Otherwise, I don't care much about it." There was a strong note of idiocy in this answer. I must have been getting tired.

"The ballet is excellent. Helene always goes when the Bolshoi comes to Brussels. Do you like ballet?"

"I don't understand much about it."

"It's a sort of nonsense, with those apparitions," he said. Then he added, "Well, fine. That's enough about Russia. You can't get worked up about things like that, or life loses its charm." And Leopold bent intently over his plate. Then he asked, "Your father plans to emigrate?"

"I hope so."

"What will he do in the West?"

"Get old. In America they'll give him a small pension."

"On the money they give, you can't have much fun."

"We'll manage," I said.

"Dodik always was a romantic. Mikhail was another. It's no wonder he died of tuberculosis. They were romantics, they were interested in art, they wrote poems. I, on the other hand, grew up entirely healthy. It's good you look like your mother. I saw a photograph of her. You resemble her a great deal."

"Yes, we're often mistaken for each other," I said.

The waiter brought the ice cream. My uncle lowered his voice and said, "If you need any money, just tell me."

"We have enough."

"But still, if you ever need money, let me know."

"Good."

"And now let's take a look around the city. I'll get a taxi."

What I liked about my uncle was the great speed at which he moved. Wherever we happened to be, he kept saying, "Very soon now we're going to have supper."

He took us to a restaurant in the center of the city, where we dined on a terrace. A Hungarian quartet played music. My uncle danced with his wife in an elegant, affectionate way. Then he noticed that Helene was tired.

35

"Let's go back to the hotel," Leopold said. "I have presents for you."

In the hotel, when he had gone off for a moment, Helene turned to me and whispered, "Don't be angry with him. He's a good man, even if he is a little primitive."

I was completely taken aback. I hadn't known she spoke Russian. She had hardly said a word, except "vodka," since we met. I would have liked to talk with her, and now it was too late.

I got home about nine, carrying a package in which a bottle of eau de Cologne for my mother made lapping noises. I had put the tie and cuff links in my pocket.

The hotel lobby was empty. Reinhardt was tapping a calculator. "I ought to get new linoleum," he said.

"Not a bad idea."

"Let's have a drink."

"With pleasure."

"The Czech student group took all the shot glasses. Can you drink out of a small paper cup?"

"Once, I had only an eyeglass case to drink from, and I managed."

Reinhardt lifted his eyebrows in admiration. We each drank down a paper cup of brandy.

"You can always sleep down here if you want to," he said, "though the couch is pretty narrow."

"Once, I even slept on a gynecological table."

Reinhardt looked at me with even greater respect. We drank again.

"I'm not going to get new linoleum," he said. "I changed my mind, since the world is doomed anyway. Humanity is in a sorry state."

"That's how it is," I said.

"Seven angels with seven trumpets have prepared themselves to sound."

Someone knocked at the door.

"Don't open it," Reinhardt said. "It's the pale horse . . . and his name that sat on him was Death."

We drank again.

"I'd better go up," I said. "Mama will start worrying."

"Be well," Reinhardt said, with some difficulty. "All hail sleep! For sleep is inactivity, and inactivity is the only moral condition known to man. All waking activity finishes in corruption. *Ciao!*"

"Good-bye," I said. "Life is absurd! It has to be absurd if I can feel closer to a German than to my own uncle!"

I spent time with Reinhardt every day after that. To tell the truth, I don't know how he got into this story. I was talking about an entirely different person, my uncle Leopold.

Yes, and Reinhardt never did get new linoleum.

I didn't see Leopold again. He went back to Brussels. For a time, we exchanged letters. Then my mother and I left for the States, and the correspondence petered out. A couple of times I've thought of calling him. What I should probably do is send him a New Year's card.

Aunt Mara

At first Aunt Mara had worked as a shipping clerk. Then she became a qualified typographer, a linotyper, if I'm not mistaken. Some time later she moved up to being a copy editor, and after that, a member of the editorial board.

And then, for her whole life, she edited other people's books.

My aunt edited the books of many remarkable writers— Tynianov, Zoshchenko, and Forsh, for example. Judging by the personal inscriptions, Zoshchenko thought very highly of her. He kept thanking her for the work they did together.

Auntie was an eye-catching woman, though there was something a little false in her torrid Armenian beauty, as there is in a mountain landscape or Lermontov's romantic verse. She was observant and witty. She had a very good memory. Many of the stories she told have stayed with me to this day. Such as this one:

She happened to meet Mikhail Zoshchenko on the street. The difficult time of official disfavor had already begun for him. Zoshchenko turned his head and quickly walked past her.

My aunt caught up with him and asked, "Why didn't you say hello to me?"

Zoshchenko grinned and said, "Forgive me. I'm trying to make it easy for my friends not to talk to me."

My aunt edited Yuri Gherman, Boris Kornilov, Seifulina, even Aleksei Tolstoi. She had something to tell about each of them.

One time Olga Forsh was at a resort for writers and was looking through the "complaint book." She found the following entry: "We keep finding all kinds of forest insects in the kasha. Not long ago at supper I came upon a large horned beetle."

"What do you think?" Forsh asked my aunt. "Was it a grievance or a note of appreciation?"

She knew a lot of stories about Aleksei Tolstoi, too. Once, Aleksei Tolstoi, who was tall and portly, was walking down the hall of the publishing house. My aunt came running from the opposite direction. She was thin and short, and she ran headfirst into Tolstoi's belly.

"Ooh!" Tolstoi said, rubbing his stomach. "And what if my eye were down there?"

My aunt knew a great many literary anecdotes.

Then, on my own, I found out that Zoshchenko had praised the use of slave labor in prison camps; that Aleksei Tolstoi was a scoundrel and a hypocrite; that chief editor

39

Nikolai Tikhonov had suggested revising all history from the moment of birth of a certain Dzhugashvili (aka Stalin); that Konstantin Fedin speculated in rugs during the evacuation; that Vera Inber had signed a petition demanding the execution of her first cousin, Leon Trotsky; that "out of curiosity" Pavlenko had gone to watch Osip Mandelstam's interrogation; that Yuri Olesha had betrayed his friend Dmitri Shostakovich; that Miroshnichenko used to beat his wife with a bicycle pump; and much more.

But what my aunt remembered for the most part were the humorous instances. I don't fault her for this. Our memory is selective, like a ballot box.

I think my aunt was a good editor. That's what I've been told by the writers she edited. Of course, I don't completely understand why an editor is really necessary. If a writer is good, it would seem an editor is not needed. If the writer is bad, no editor can save him. This has always seemed self-evident.

I know how my aunt worked with authors. Sometimes I was even present. For example, she would say, "Yura, there are four places in this passage where the word 'dank' appears."

"You're absolutely right," Yuri Pavlovich Gherman would say. "How is it I didn't notice that myself?"

Nevertheless, I still believe a writer doesn't need an editor—not even a good writer. And a bad one, still less.

Take the following historical example: Dostoyevski wrote a sentence in one of his novels that went, "Beside it stood a round table of oval form." Someone reading the work in manuscript said, "Fyodor Mikhailovich, you've made a slip here. It should be corrected."

Dostoyevski thought for a moment and said, "Leave it as it is."

In his early works, Nikolai Gogol used to use the word "stucko." Once, the writer Aksakov said to him, "Why do you write 'stucko'?"

"Why, what's wrong with it?" Gogol asked.

"It should be 'stucco'. "

"I don't think so," Gogol said.

"Look it up in the dictionary."

So they got out the dictionary and looked it up, and there it was—"stucco." From then on, Gogol invariably wrote "stucco," but he didn't correct the mistake in new editions of his earlier works.

Why? Why didn't Dostoyevski want to eliminate a glaring error? Why did Alexandre Dumas call his novel *The Three Musketeers*, though clearly there are four of them? There are hundreds of instances like this in literature. What becomes apparent is that the errors, the inaccuracies, are in some way dear to the author, and thus to the reader as well.

How can you correct Rozanov's line "We never wept anything like that"?

If it were up to me, I wouldn't even correct typographical errors without the consent of an author. And certainly not punctuation. Punctuation is something every writer invents for himself.

I think my aunt was a good editor, or, rather, she was a good person, full of goodwill and intelligence.

Personally, I have never met a good editor, though there were many fine people among those I did meet. Actually, there *was* one time I met a good editor. It was at Lenfilm, I think, and it was a certain woman named Hellie Rummo.

She was Estonian and barely spoke Russian, and her weak command of the language gave her pronouncements a special clarity. She would say, "The scenario is good. So they won't take it."

In the 1960s I began writing short stories. I showed my work to my aunt. She found hundreds of mistakes in my stories: of style, spelling, and punctuation.

She said things like, "In this passage you write, 'the kinship of silence and frost.' It's inaccurate. Frost and silence are two different kinds of phenomena. You should write, 'In the forest it was cold and quiet.' Without making it fancy . . ."

"Why do you say 'in the forest'?" I asked in surprise. "The action takes place in a penal isolation cell."

"Ah, yes," she would say.

Those were the years that she was put in charge of the editorial board that chose new manuscripts for publication. As a result, many good writers were published.

Among others, Joseph Brodsky submitted a manuscript to the board. My aunt did not accept it. She called his poems "the ravings of a madman." (Actually, Brodsky's poems do have something of that, too.)

My aunt was a member of the Party. I don't fault her for this either. Many worthy and honest people joined the ranks of the Communist Party. They were not to blame. They simply wanted to live better, hold higher positions.

Of course, my aunt took it very badly when they persecuted Anna Akhmatova and Zoshchenko. And when they hounded Boris Pasternak to his grave, she became so upset that she even got sick. She said, "This step is politically unsound. We will lose our prestige in the West. We are in danger of canceling out the achievements of the Twentieth Party Congress. . . ."

Over many years, my aunt collected a very fine library. The majority of the books had personal inscriptions from the authors, often touching and tender ones. Valentin Pikul's colorful inscription began with the words "To the midwife of our souls . . ."

The inscription that the science fiction writer Gansovski wrote said: "Across time and space, I give my hand to you!" Not long ago it became known that Gansovski was an informer, who denounced his own friends.

Pikul also distinguished himself in this field. At the trial of Kiril Vladimirovich Uspensky, he addressed the defendant this way: "Kiril! All of us here wish only what is good for you, but you continue to lie!" Since the trial took place during a time when liberalism was at its height, Uspensky was given only five years in labor camp. Pikul got an apartment in Riga.

In her later years, my aunt read a great deal. She didn't reread any of the books with inscriptions. Beside her bed, instead, lay volumes of Akhmatova, Pasternak, Baratyn-ski . . .

When my aunt died, her library was sold at once. To get it ready for sale, her son and his wife tore out the pages with the inscriptions. Otherwise it would have been more awkward to sell the books.

Not long before this, my aunt had read me some lines of poetry:

> Midway by now on the journey of this life,
> While I still think that I move mountains,
> That I plow the fields, that I water valleys,
> While life's already far beyond the midpoint . . .

"Verses of a certain poetess," she said with a smile.

I think she wrote them herself. The lines are clumsy, of course. The first line is lifted from Dante. Still, in spite of everything, the poem touched me.

> Midway by now on the journey of this life,
> While I still think that I move mountains . . .

My aunt was mistaken. Her life was coming to its close. The errors could no longer be corrected.

Uncle Aron

The biography of my aunt's husband, Aron, zigzags like the history of the Soviet Union itself. First he was a *Gymnasium* student, then a radical university student, then, for a short time, a Red Army soldier. Next, strange as it sounds, he joined the White Poles fighting the Red Army. Then he became a Red Army man again, this time out of political conviction.

When the Civil War ended, Uncle Aron entered a workers' university program. When the Party tried the New Economic Policy, he became a NEPman and, it seems, got temporarily rich. Then he worked at dispossessing the kulaks. Next he helped purge the ranks of the Party. Then he himself was purged for having been a NEPman.

At that meeting, my uncle delivered a speech. He said: "If

45

you expel me, I will be obliged to tell my wife, and she'll hit the roof. It's up to you."

The comrades thought about it and decided: "Expel!"

Later, it is true, he was reinstated. The main thing was, he didn't have to do time in prison.

He went into management; he became the director of something, or maybe the deputy director of a division of something.

My uncle adored Stalin—adored him the way one adores a wayward son, knowing his shortcomings. He collected phonograph records with all the speeches of the Generalissimo and kept them in red albums that were tied with laces and had a relief portrait of the Leader on the front.

When Stalin was exposed as a villain, my uncle was sincerely grieved. Then he became infatuated with Georgi Malenkov. He liked to remark that Malenkov was an educated man, an engineer.

When Malenkov was removed from power, he fell in love with Nikolai Bulganin. Bulganin had the appearance of a backwoods, pre-Revolutionary police chief. Perhaps, since my uncle came from the provinces himself, he honestly fell in love with Bulganin as someone who reminded him of his childhood idols.

Then he fell in love with Khrushchev, and when Khrushchev was removed from power, my uncle lost some of his ability to love. He got sick of always suffering losses on his emotional investments.

It was then that he decided to fall in love with Lenin. Lenin had died long before and could not be removed from power. It was close to impossible even to smear his name. This meant the love could not decline in value.

At the same time, though, my uncle somehow came loose

ideologically. He fell in love with Lenin but also with Solzhenitsyn. Sakharov, too—mainly because he had helped invent the hydrogen bomb in the Soviet Union and then hadn't become a drunk but fought for the truth.

In the last years of his life, he was practically a dissident, but a moderate one. He never for an instant tolerated the anti-Communist, pro-Nazi Vlasovites. He revered Solzhenitsyn selectively.

Brezhnev he did not like. He regarded Brezhnev as a temporary phenomenon, which didn't turn out to be the case.

My uncle used to send Brezhnev anonymous letters. He wrote them in the savings bank in violet ink, using his left hand and printing in block letters. These letters were brief. They might say: "Where are you leading Russia, monster?" Signed, "General Sviridov." Or, "The Baikal-Amur Mainline is a complete fiction!" Signed, "General Kolyuzhny." Sometimes he employed more artistic forms:

> "Thy brows
> Crave blood!"

Signed, "General Nechiporenko."

My uncle wished to return to the roots of Leninism; I did not. This was the source of endless arguments. The level of the polemic was not high.

"A provocateur, a syphilitic, and a German spy," I said of Lenin.

"Blasphemer and blockhead!" my uncle said to me.

We touched on a rather narrow range of themes: lynchings, the decline of morals, the Vietnam epic. . . .

My uncle would get terribly angry. "Fascist!" he would shout at me. "Dyed-in-the-wool Vlasovite!"

And then, suddenly, my uncle was on his deathbed. More

accurately, he got very sick and decided it was time for him to die. He was seventy-six years old.

"I want to see Seryozha," he told his wife.

I came at once. Uncle lay propped up on pillows, thin and pale. He asked everyone else to leave the room.

"Sergei," he said very quietly, "I'm dying."

I said nothing.

"I'm not afraid of death." He paused for a moment and then went on. "I've made honest mistakes. . . . I've felt anguish over the wrong steps I've taken. Here is what I have understood: The holy tenets I upheld all my life have turned out to be false. I've cracked up ideologically."

He asked for water. I lifted a cup to his lips.

"Sergei," he said, "I always scolded you, but it was only because I was afraid. I was afraid they would arrest you. You're very unrestrained. . . . I criticized you, but deep down I agreed with you. You should understand me. Forty years of that"—and here Uncle used a very dirty word—"Party. Sixty years under this"—here he repeated the word—"system . . ."

"Please calm down," I said.

". . . have turned me into a whore," he said, finishing the sentence. He had to make an effort to go on. "You were always right. I only argued because I was afraid for you. Forgive me."

He started to cry. I felt very sorry for him. Just then, an ambulance arrived and they took my uncle to the hospital.

They took him to an ordinary hospital. My aunt had thought he would be taken to the Sverdlovsk Party Hospital.

"But you're an Old Bolshevik," she kept saying.

"No," he said, differing. "I am not an Old Bolshevik."

"How is that?"

"The term 'Old Bolshevik' has a particular, concrete meaning. An Old Bolshevik is someone who entered the Party before 1935. I entered a bit later."

This was news to my aunt. "You mean to say you're not an Old Bolshevik?"

"No."

"But still," she said, "surely they owe you something?"

"It's possible," my uncle agreed. "It's possible they owe me something. An apple, for example . . ."

So he went to an ordinary hospital. When the admitting doctor examined him, my uncle asked, "Doctor, were you at the front?"

"Yes," the doctor said, "I was at the front."

"So was I," my uncle said. "So tell me honestly, as one front-line soldier to another, will I be in the hospital long?"

"If all goes well, a month," the doctor answered.

"And if all goes not so well," my uncle said with a smile, "considerably less?"

He was in the hospital for about three weeks, and then he came home. I went over to visit him right away.

He seemed sad and quiet, as if he had attained some higher wisdom. However, when I brought up Che Guevara in our conversation, Uncle grew alert. I said of Guevara, "An adventurer and a gangster."

"And you're a social parasite and a blockhead!" he shot back. Then, with enormous animation, "Show me one good idea that exists outside of communism!"

At this point, he suddenly interrupted his own speech. He must have remembered our deathbed conversation. He gave me a guilty look. I said nothing.

From that time on, we saw each other often, and invariably we quarreled. Uncle railed against rock music, the defector Baryshnikov, and General Andrei Vlasov. I took stands against socialized medicine, "Swan Lake," and Feliks Dzerzhinski.

Then he fell ill again. "Ask Seryozha to come," he told his wife.

I came at once. Uncle looked pale and shrunken. The stool near the head of his bed was covered with medicine bottles. His dentures in a glass gave off a rosy, intimate glow.

"Sergei," he said in a muffled voice. I stroked his hand. "I have an enormous favor to ask you. Give me your word you'll do it."

I nodded.

"Smother me," he said.

In dismay, I said nothing.

"I'm sick of living. I don't believe communism can be built in one country. I've slid into the swamp of Trotskyism."

"Don't think about it," I said.

"Are you prepared to do what I ask of you? I can see that you're hesitating. I could, of course, take twenty sleeping pills. But alas, they're not sure to cause death—and what if I woke up paralyzed? I would become an even heavier burden to everyone. That's why I absolutely have to turn to you for help."

"Stop it," I said, "stop it."

"Don't think I won't show my gratitude," my uncle said. "I'll will you my set of the complete works of Lenin. Then you can take them to the recycling plant and exchange them for a really good edition of *Pinocchio*. But I'm not giving you anything unless you smother me."

"Stop it," I said.

"There's nothing but malice and stupidity all around us," he said. "There's no truth."

"Calm down."

"Do you know what torments me?" he said. "When we lived in Novorossisk there was a fence—a tall brown fence—near our house. I walked by that fence every day. And I don't know what was behind it. I never asked. I didn't think it was important. How senselessly and stupidly I've lived my life! So this means you refuse?"

"Stop it," I said.

Uncle turned away from me and would not talk any more.

Two weeks later, he got well. We went back to our terrible quarrels.

"Blockhead!" he would shout. "You refuse to understand anything! Communism may have been compromised by mediocrities, but the idea is as brilliant as ever! No wonder millions of people believe in the ideology of communism!"

"*Who* believes in it?" I would say. "Not one person who thinks logically and clearly."

"So you think they *don't* believe in it?" my uncle said, red in the face. "They don't believe in it and say nothing? You're trying to tell me there are nothing but hypocrites all around us?"

"It's not necessary to believe in an ideology," I said. "You can take it or leave it. It's like prison: you like it, you don't like it, but you stay put."

"Blockhead!" he would shout. "Vlasovite! Black marketeer!"

A small portrait of Solzhenitsyn hung near the head of his bed. He took it down whenever guests came.

These scenes were repeated again and again. Uncle would get sick, then get well. We would quarrel and then make peace. Years passed. He became truly old. I was very attached to him.

As I said, my uncle's biography reflects the whole recent history of our country, of our beloved and awful land.

Then my uncle actually did die. A pity, and that tall brown fence gives me no peace.

Mother

From early childhood, my upbringing was politically tendentious. My mother, for instance, had an abiding contempt for Stalin that she willingly and publicly expressed. True, she did so in a rather original way, by insisting, "A Georgian cannot possibly be a decent man." She had been taught this in the Armenian quarter of Tbilisi, the Georgian capital, where she grew up.

My father, on the other hand, felt great esteem for the Leader, though he was the one who had good reason to hate Stalin, especially since his father had been shot.

Perhaps my father did hate tyranny, but at the same time he felt awe for its grand scale. Anyway, the fact that Stalin was a murderer was well known to my parents, and to my parents' friends. It was just about the only thing they talked about at home.

There's one thing I don't understand. How come my ordinary parents knew everything, while Ilya Eherenburg didn't?

By the age of six, I myself knew that Stalin had been responsible for the death of my grandfather, and by the time I finished school, I knew most everything else. I knew that the newspapers printed lies. That ordinary people abroad lived better lives, were materially better off and more carefree. That to be a Party member was shameful but to one's advantage.

This doesn't mean I was a thoughtful or reflective boy; not at all. Just the opposite. It was simply that I was told these things by my parents. More precisely, by my mother. My father had little to do with my upbringing, mostly because he and my mother had divorced early in my life.

Mother and I lived in a revolting communal apartment. The long, gloomy corridor led, metaphysically, to the toilet. The wallpaper by the telephone was covered with doodles, leaving a depressing chronicle of the communal unconscious. Zoya Svistunova, an unmarried mother, always drew wildflowers. Gordei Borisovich Ovsyannikov, a life-loving engineer, carefully shaded in the contours of female buttocks. Dumb Colonel Tikhomirov drew military emblems. Kharin, who worked as a technician, drew bottles and shot glasses. Mme. Zhuravlyova, a singer in touring musical revues, drew treble clefs that looked like ears. I drew pistols and swords.

Our apartment was hardly typical. Its inhabitants were, for the most part, members of the intelligentsia. There were no open quarrels. No one spit in his neighbor's soup (though one can't be completely sure). This didn't mean that all was peaceful and decorous. An undeclared, underhanded war never subsided. A stewpot full of mutual irritation simmered and bubbled quietly.

My mother worked as a copy editor, on three different shifts. Sometimes she went to bed late, sometimes early. Sometimes she had to sleep during the day. Children ran up and down the hallway. Tikhomirov's army boots thundered by. Hapless Kharin dragged his bicycle to his room. Zhuravlyova rehearsed her songs.

My mother could not get enough sleep. And her job carried a lot of responsibility. Stalin was still alive then, and a single misprint in a newspaper could mean prison for the person held responsible. When it comes to printing newspapers, disaster can follow the omission of one letter. The word that results may be either obscene or, even worse, anti-Soviet (and sometimes both).

For example, take a headline like "An order from the Commander in Chief." "Commander in Chief" is such a long word, all you had to do was drop the letter "l" in Russian and you got the equivalent of "Commander in Shit." This is what seemed to happen most often. Or, by dropping one letter, you got "Communists condemn the decisions of the Party" (instead of "consider" the decisions). Or, one omitted letter turned "Bolshevik cohorts" into "Bolshevik labor camps."

As everyone knows, the only truth in our newspapers is in the misprints.

For the last twenty years, people have no longer been shot for such errors. My mother, though, was a copy editor thirty years ago. She never got enough sleep at home. For days on end she would fight agonizing battles for quiet.

Once, when she couldn't take it anymore, she hung a despairing sign on her doors: "A half-corpse (*polutrup*) is resting inside. Silence, please!"

And suddenly it became truly quiet in the apartment, something unexpected and unusual. Tikhomirov wandered through the hallways in his socks. He kept grabbing everyone by the arm and hissing, "Quiet! A political instructor (*politruk*) is spending the night in Dovlatova's room."

The Colonel was glad that Mama had at last found personal happiness, and, what was even better, with a politically mature comrade. Besides, a political instructor inspired some alarm. He might turn out to be higher in rank than Tikhomirov himself.

The quiet lasted one week, before they realized their mistake.

My mother was born in Tbilisi. In her childhood she studied music. A Russian woman gave her lessons without charging the family any money.

It was a happy life. In the first place, it was the South. Second, there were four children in the family. Her sister Mara was mischievous and clever. Her sister Aniela was a nasty spoiled brat. Little brother Roman was always getting into fights and was a bully, besides. My mother seemed to be the most ordinary among the children.

Schopenhauer writes somewhere that people do not change. So then how was it that Aunt Mara became an exacting literary editor? How did Uncle Roman, the ruffian and bully, become an ordinary bureaucrat? How did nasty Aniela grow up into the kindest, most honest and unassuming person, so irreproachable that it's too boring to write about her? And how did my mother end up living in the capitalist jungles, reading émigré literary journals and breaking into Georgian, out of helplessness, in the supermarket?

I really know very little about her youth. In the 1930s all the sisters left Georgia and settled in Leningrad. Aunt Aniela entered the department of foreign languages at the university. Aunt Mara went to work for a publishing house. My mother applied simultaneously to the conservatory and to a theater institute. She took the entrance exam for both places at about the same time—you were allowed to do that in those days—and both institutions accepted her. She says they accepted everyone. A new, nonclass intelligentsia was being created.

She chose to enter the theater institute. I myself think it was the wrong choice. Generally speaking, one should avoid the artistic professions. If you can't avoid them, then it's another matter; there's no way out. It means you didn't choose it, but, rather, it chose you.

My mother worked in the theater for a few years. In the few reviews that I've read, she got good notices. The group of actors that she worked with respected her, as they say. The actor Bernatski liked to say, "It would be nice to punch Donat right in the puss! . . . Only I would be sorry for Nora."

Donat is my father. His reaction to Bernatski's statement was, "If you have a face like Zhenya Bernatski's, you shouldn't leave the house."

Then I was born. My father and mother often quarreled. Then they separated, but I stayed on.

Mama could no longer be bothered with out-of-town guest appearances, and so she gave up the theater. And she was right to do it. I knew many of her friends who stayed in the theater till their deaths. Theirs was a world of wounded vanity, trampled personal ambitions, of endless put-downs of other people's acting. They were all impoverished, vindictive, and envious.

Mama became a copy editor, even an excellent copy editor. She obviously had a talent for the work. She had absolutely no knowledge of grammar, but she possessed a real flair for editing. It can happen sometimes.

I think she was a born copy editor. She had—if you can put it this way—an ethical sense of spelling. She might say of someone, for example, "You know, he is one of those people who write 'in general' with a hyphen." This signified a low point in moral development.

Of someone who was inane, frivolous, but nice, she would say, "The kind that writes 'enough' with f's . . ."

My mother worked from morning till night. I ate a great deal. I kept growing. In order to feed me well, my mother ate almost nothing but potatoes. Until the age of seventeen I was absolutely convinced that she preferred potatoes to all other food. (Here in New York it has been proven definitively that this is not so.)

Even though it was crowded with people, life in our apartment was very dull. Real events were extremely rare. Once, Colonel Tikhomirov had a visit from a distant relative by the name of Suchkov, a grown, clumsy lad from the settlement of Dulevo.

"Uncle," he said, having just arrived, "render me material assistance in the form of three rubles. Otherwise I may take the wrong road."

"You've taken one wrong step already," Tikhomirov said, "since you've asked for money. But I have no money, so don't count on me."

The nephew sat down on a communal chest and burst into tears, and there he sat till lunchtime. Finally my mother said, "Come in. You must be hungry."

"I've been hungry a long time," Suchkov said.

Somehow he settled in with us. He ate huge meals and

then went walking around Leningrad. Evenings, he would drink tea and watch television. It was the first time he had ever seen TV. Colonel Tikhomirov maintained a neutral stance, but he stopped greeting my mother when he met her.

Finally, my mother asked Suchkov, "Volodya, what exactly are your plans?"

Suchkov sighed. "I'd like to get some money together for textbooks . . . for firewood. . . . I want to study," he said in conclusion. Then he added sternly, "Otherwise I fear I may take the wrong road."

My mother borrowed fifteen rubles for Suchkov from a neighbor and bought him a train ticket back to Dulevo. Forty minutes before his train departed, Suchkov asked for some tea. He drank cup after cup, dissolving limitless amounts of sugar, first in tea and then in boiling water, as if he wished to exhaust the unexpected bounty of his surroundings.

"Careful, don't be late," my mother said anxiously.

Suchkov wiped his face with a newspaper and kept saying, "Something makes me want water. . . ."

Then my mother could contain herself no longer. "So then go and drown yourself!" she shouted.

The nonrelative frowned. He gave my mother a look full of reproach. There was a painful pause. "How petty you are, Nonna Stepanovna," he said to her, getting everything wrong in one shot: her name, patronymic, and the facts of the matter. He stood up, threw a tragic look at the remaining salami and sugar, squared his shoulders, and started off down the wrong road.

That's how we lived.

I, too, provided a constant source of grief for my mother. At first I did badly at school, badly and unevenly: at times I might suddenly become a participant in some sort of regional chemistry competition and at other times it would be nothing but F's. Even in literature.

In 1954 I was a winner in an all-Union competition of young poets. There were three of us who won—Lenya Dyatilov, Sasha Makarov, and me. In his more mature years, Lenya Dyatilov took to drink. Makarov became a translator of the languages of the Komi people. As for me, it's never been clear, exactly, just what my occupation is. But back then we were the champions. The prizes were awarded to us by the children's book writer Samuil Yakovlevich Marshak.

The competition came and went, and a long series of F's began again. These I got due not to independence of mind but to being dumb. I shamelessly copied the primitive compositions of my classmates. I never got through *The Young Guard,* and now it's certain I never will. In a word, I was a bad student. My friends were the school rabble. To make things worse, I smoked and drank occasionally.

At the university I also did poorly. To make up for it, I kept threatening my mother with marriage, God knows to whom.

Then I was drafted into the army. I did badly as a soldier, too. I had no military style or bearing. I managed to serve the whole time without polishing my dog tag once.

Finally I was discharged. I began to work for large daily newspapers. I kept changing jobs. On top of everything else, I began writing short stories. Naturally these stories were not published. I started drinking more. Masquerading as an unrecognized genius somehow made existence easier.

Appropriate friends appeared: bearded, enigmatic, and gloomy. In addition, they didn't wash their hands after using the toilet. My mother, though, had very strict ideas on this score, maybe even stricter than her ideas about spelling.

If a friend went to use the toilet, my mother would stop whatever she was doing. From the changing timbres of flowing water, she would ascertain whether he was washing his hands or not. She would wait and listen carefully. At first it was quiet. Then, with a powerful rumble, the water descended from the water tank. Then right away the door would open and slam—which meant he hadn't washed.

My mother would start hinting and fussing about. "Probably there isn't any soap left in there. Can I get you a clean towel?" She deluged the friend with leading questions. Stubbornly she tried to prod him toward better personal hygiene.

The friend would answer, "Don't worry yourself about it. Everything's as it should be." And some only raised their eyebrows in amazement.

If the friend lingered, if the thundering torrent changed to the murmur of the water faucet, my mother burst into a smile. She listened for the silence that followed, caught the rustle of the towel.

To such a guest, my mother offered coffee. She conversed with him about Rachmaninoff. But this rarely happened. They were, after all, my friends.

They didn't get published either. Their reaction to this situation was generally neurotic and noisy. They drank fortified wine and regarded one another as geniuses. Almost all my friends were geniuses, and some were even geniuses in several areas at once. Sasha Kondratov, for instance, was a genius at mathematics, linguistics, poetry, physics, and church art. On his pinky he proudly wore a homemade tin ring in the shape of a skull.

My mother sympathized with my friends, fed them, and listened to their boastful, crazy outpourings. She took the role of audience. (How can you have a genius without an audience, a mob?) She intentionally asked naïve questions. She supplied, as it were, the questions shouted from the floor of a full house.

"So tell me, is Paustovski talented?" she would ask.

"Paustovski? Manure!" her partner in conversation would say, in an academic tone.

"And Kataev?"

"Total manure . . ."

In 1976 three of my stories were published in the West. From then on, publishing in the Soviet Union was closed to me (as actually, it had been all along). I was simultaneously proud and terrified.

My friends had complicated reactions. Some warned, "Wait and see; they'll lock you up. They'll cook up some criminal offense, and then it's good-bye!"

Others put it like this: "So they published you, so what? In the West most books get published in minuscule numbers. Nobody there will notice. And here all your roads will be blocked."

The third kind of reaction was condemnation. "A writer ought to publish in his native land."

And only my mother kept saying, "I'm so glad that you're finally getting published!"

Then the troubles started.

I was fired from every place I worked. I couldn't even get hack jobs. I managed to set up a job as a watchman on some idiotic barge—and they threw me out of there, too.

I began drinking heavily. My wife and daughter left for the

West. The two of us were left alone—actually, the three of us, Mama, me, and Glasha, the dog.

The standard hounding began. I was accused of breaking the Criminal Code on three counts: social parasitism, insubordination to the authorities, and possessing "other non-firearm" weapons. All three charges were false.

The police appeared practically every day. But at this point I, too, took defensive measures. We lived in a fifth-floor walk-up. A neighbor on our floor, Genadi Sakhno, was always leaning out of his window. He was an alcoholic journalist and, like many lushes, a man of blinding nobility of character. He spent days at a time guzzling port wine at his window.

If he spotted the police walking up to our building entrance, Genadi would pick up the telephone. "The whores are coming," he would say laconically. And I would immediately bolt the door. The police would leave with nothing. Genadi Sakhno would get an honestly earned ruble.

That's how we got by.

My mother kept repeating, "I'm so glad that you're finally being published."

Then I was suddenly arrested and put in Kalyaevski Prison. I don't much feel like writing about it in detail. I'll say only this about it: I didn't like being in jail. Before then, I had sometimes said to my older first cousin, "You did time in labor camp, I served as a guard in a labor camp—what difference does it make? It was the same thing." After my arrest, I understood that it wasn't the same thing at all. But I still don't feel like writing about the details.

Then suddenly I was released.

It was suggested that I leave the country—emigrate. I agreed.

I didn't even ask my mother if she was ready to make the journey out with me. I was amazed to learn that there were families who took months to make up their minds, sometimes with tragic results.

We also didn't have any problem with Glasha. We just had to pay some money to get her out, two rubles sixty kopecks per kilo of her weight. Glasha was valued at slightly more than ham and much cheaper than a good steak.

Now we live in New York, and we'll never part. Just as we never parted before, even when I went away for a long time.

Father

My father always liked to cut a figure, so it's no wonder he became an actor. Life appeared to him as grand theater. Stalin reminded him of the villains in Shakespeare's plays. The people suffered in silence, just as they did in Pushkin's *Boris Godunov.*

Vladivostok was a theatrical city, not unlike Odessa. Foreign sailors brawled in the port restaurants. You might hear African music in the city parks. On the main street, the Svetlanka, dandies strolled about wearing poison-green pants. There were cafés in which people discussed the latest suicide over unrequited love.

It was all neither comedy nor tragedy, but drama. In the end, good triumphed over evil. Base impulses were counterbalanced by high passions. Happiness and grief ran in the same harness. The main character would stand revealed in all his stature.

The main character was none other than my father himself.

I think my father had a certain talent. With no ear for music, he sang comic songs; as a clumsy adolescent, he danced. He could pass himself off as brave. All these things involved performance.

My father wrote poetry, too. His poems were always about the death wish. I take this as evidence of his overabundant life force. Poetry attracted him as one of the elements of theatrical performance. He fell in love with tennis in the same way: Tennis players wore good-looking sports clothes and the points were called in English.

Like many young people from the provinces, my father and his brothers were drawn to the great cities. Donat, my father, went off to Leningrad to perfect his dramatic gifts. Mikhail followed after him. Swashbuckling Leopold surfaced in Shanghai.

My father entered the theater institute and went through rather quickly as a representative of the new intelligentsia. He became a director. Everything was going well. He was hired by the Academic Theater. He worked with such top actors as Vivyen and Tolubeyev. I've seen good reviews of the plays he directed. Of course, at that time, there were plenty of bad reviews of the great Meyerhold's productions.

Then anxious times began. My parents' friends suddenly began to disappear.

My mother cursed Stalin for what was happening. My father judged things differently. After all, he remarked, only the most ordinary people were disappearing. And along with their good qualities, each one of them had grave shortcomings. In each of them, if you really thought about it, there was something negative, something that allowed you to come to terms with the loss.

When the police took away the man who lived on the floor below us—Lyabin, the choirmaster—my father reminded everyone that Lyabin was an anti-Semite. When they arrested the philologist Roginski, it was revealed that Roginski drank. Zatsepin, my father's coworker at the theater, was not tactful in his dealings with women. Sidelnikov, the makeup man, preferred men altogether. And Shapiro, the cinematographer, conducted himself with amazing assurance for a Jew. All this was to say that a drama was being played out in which each fatal flaw was punished.

Then Grandpa Isaak was arrested—just like that. He disappeared. For my father, it was completely unexpected, inasmuch as Grandpa was a manifestly good man. Of course, Grandpa had weaknesses, too, but very few. Anyway, the faults were one-hundred-percent private in nature. For instance, he ate a lot.

The drama was turning into tragedy. My father went to pieces. He suddenly saw that death lurked somewhere nearby, that the main character was imperiled, as in a Shakespearean tragedy.

Then my father himself was forced to leave his job in the theater. As he should have been, in keeping with his own theories: a Jew, with a father who had been shot, with a brother living abroad, and so on.

Father began writing for variety shows. He wrote light sketches, satirical songs, skits, and comedy routines. He became a professional gag writer and would spend days on end thinking up jokes. As everyone knows, such activity completely drains you of good spirits.

I remember one of his routines by heart; it will stay with me forever.

> By chance I saw
> The head of our food store;
> This manager's strong as an ox;
> The only thing is,
> It's now been ten years
> Since our store has carried lox.

I remember, when I first heard these crazy lines, asking my father what they were supposed to mean. Father got angry and shouted in a high, tragic voice, "You're not getting the point! You just don't have any sense of humor!"

Then he got to thinking, went off by himself for about forty minutes. He came back out of his study and triumphantly recited his new version:

> Our food-store manager is quite a guy,
> Like a pickle fresh out of brine;
> Only, it's been a good ten years
> Since pickles in the store appeared.

"So, what do you think?" he asked.

"They sell pickles everywhere you look," my mother said.

"Well, so what?"

"So, then, it's not true to life."

"What's not true to life? What exactly is not true to life?"

"That line about no pickles in the store. It would make more sense if you wrote about beef salami."

My father clutched his hair and started screaming, "What has beef salami got to do with it? Don't talk to me as if I were some housewife! I have no interest in the vulgar details of your existence! Not true to life!" Father repeated as he locked the door to his study.

I knew he was writing lyric poems then. I read them twenty years later. Unfortunately, I didn't like them.

His music-hall lead-ins were better. For example, the master of ceremonies would come out and announce: "Now Rubina Kalantaryan will sing the Mexican song 'Crimson Flower.' The lyrics go: 'Juanito gave me a crimson flower. "I'm a poor man," said Juanito, "and cannot give you a necklace of pearls. So at least take from me this flower!" . . . "Juanito," I said, "you've given me something more valuable than a pearl necklace. You have given me your love!" ' And so—Rubina Kalantaryan! The Mexican song 'Crimson Flower!' The song will be performed *in Russian!*"

I remember people laughing in the theater.

Father was a romantic-looking man. His face had an imposing quality, even though it wasn't based on anything and was a little overdone. He looked youthful and fairly elegant and yet, at the same time, like one of the flophouse dwellers from Gorky's *The Lower Depths.* He looked like a cross between Pushkin and an American on unemployment.

Naturally, Father drank now and then—perhaps it was no more than others did, but it was somehow more noticeable. In a word, he was regarded as a lush, and unjustly so. His theatricality shook people up a little even when he was sober.

He was surrounded by an assortment of shady characters, even though he himself was entirely honest. And in matters involving money he was absolutely scrupulous.

I was always impressed by his tolerance with regard to other people. The person who forced him out of his job in the theater was someone my mother hated for the rest of her life; Father, on the other hand, had a friendly drink with him a month later.

Father was a purveyor of puns and jokes. Unfortunately, Mother possessed a sense of humor. Two more dissimilar people could hardly exist, that much is clear.

Like all frivolous men, Father was a kindhearted person. Mother was outspoken and sharp-tongued. Her exceptional honesty allowed for no compromises. Her slightest gesture took on the quality of self-sacrifice. In the merciless light of her moral purity, my father's shortcomings stood out catastrophically. They separated when I was eight years old.

So my father lived through the cult of personality, through war, evacuation. Then divorce, hackwork, women . . . Evenings at the theater folk's restaurant . . .

The years went by. I was growing up. The Great Leader was debunked. Grandpa's name was rehabilitated, as they say. My father again took heart. It seemed to him that the third and final act of the life drama was beginning, and now Good would finally triumph. One might even say it already had.

He married for the second time. A nice young woman technician had fallen in love with him. She may have taken him for a brilliant eccentric. That kind of thing sometimes happens.

In short, things were getting better. The play had regained its lost momentum. The long-breached rules of classical drama were being restored.

And then what happened? Nothing much. The country was ruled by a bunch of nondescript, faceless leaders. A depressing, colorless uniformity held sway in the arts. On the other hand, father would point out, people were not being shot, or even imprisoned. Well, they were sent to prison, yes, but not so often. At any rate, if they were, it was for some concrete action, or at least for some imprudent public remark. That is, for a reason. Not the way things used to be.

Nevertheless, it had been better under Stalin. Under Stalin, they would publish books, and then shoot the authors. Now they didn't shoot writers and they didn't publish books. Jewish theaters weren't being closed down; there just weren't any.

The heirs of Stalin disappointed my father. They lacked grandeur, brilliance, theatricality. My father was ready to accept tyranny, but the tyranny of an Oriental despot, colorful and rather wild.

He was convinced that Stalin had been buried improperly. He should never have been buried like an ordinary mortal. It wasn't proper to write about his illnesses, about a hemorrhage in the brain, and on top of that to publish some inappropriate urinalysis.

They should just have announced that Stalin had disappeared, or, more simply, that he had ascended. And everyone would have believed it. Then the great legend could have continued. In what way was Stalin inferior to that young fellow from Nazareth? As things were now, all you had was a bunch of discontented, overfed types standing by the mausoleum. Dressed-up pensioners, judging by the looks of them.

Life was becoming increasingly lackluster and monotonous. Even villainy took on a kind of banal, abject quality. Goodness was transformed into apathy. People would say: "So-and-so is a good person, he doesn't inform on anyone."

I don't remember my father being interested in life. What interested him was theater. Behind the riot of his words, actions, and thoughts one could hardly make out the innocent, impractical soul.

A conversation he once had with a writer named Markovsky has always stayed with me. It seems Markovsky had had a lot to drink and said, "Can you imagine, Donat—I informed on people."

Father blew up. "I'll never shake your hand again!"

Markovsky wanted to clarify what he had said. "I never reported good people. Only bad ones."

My father thought about this for a moment and then said, "Just who appointed you judge, Arkady? What does that mean—bad people, good people? Why should it be decided by you, of all people? Who are you, Jesus Christ?"

Markovsky tried to explain again. "Bad people are the ones who never buy dinner for their friends . . . people who drink alone. . . ."

"Well, that's all right, then," my father said.

In those years he was practically the dean of a music school where, on his initiative, students could specialize in variety-show performance. Those were the students he taught himself. He would call his graduate students disciples, in the manner of Pythagoras. The disciples loved him for his democratic ways.

But some rather peculiar things went on in that institution. One of the other teachers wrote a letter of denunciation, charging my father with corrupting the students, going to restaurants with them, chasing after young girls, and so on. The denunciation was unsigned.

Father was summoned to the director's office. The calamitous sheet of paper was shown to him. Father pulled out a magnifying glass and asked, "Would you permit me to look at this closely?"

He bent over the paper. After a minute he began muttering

quietly: "So . . . Pressure on the capital letters: dark-haired . . . Space between 'b' and hard sign: narrow eyes . . . An unclosed oval: chain-smoker . . . 'R' that ends up looking like an 'e': shoe size 43 . . . Good . . . Short flourish under the 'g': mustache . . . Ragged crossbar in the capital 'H': broken tooth."

Then my father stood up and exclaimed triumphantly, "This was written by Shurik Boguslavski!"

The anonymous writer was exposed. My father's longtime hobby, graphology, had yielded dazzling results. Boguslavski confessed.

A meeting was organized, and my father stood up and said, "Shurik! Alexander Ghermanovich! How is it possible that you, a member of the Party, could do such a thing?"

When he told me this later, I said to my father, "The fact that Boguslavski is a Party member goes perfectly with his writing a denunciation. That's just what *is* logical and natural."

But he continued to fret. "A member of the Communist Party . . . A figure invested with the trust of the people . . ."

My father had within him a deep and stubborn lack of understanding of the way things are.

Meanwhile, events took a rather dim turn. My father's daughter by his second marriage fell in love with a young computer programmer named Lenya, and after marrying, they prepared to emigrate. And, since my stories were being published in the West, I was hesitating between Paris and prison.

As a crowning touch, my father was again forced out of his job. "So that's that," I said. "We'll leave together."

"To go where?"

73

"Anywhere you want. Into the capitalist jungles."

"And what am I supposed to do there?"

"Nothing. Grow old."

My father almost blew up. Whoever heard of such a thing—leaving the stage in the last act? Three minutes before the final curtain and the applause?

What could I tell him? That we weren't onstage but in orchestra seats? That the lights had come up for intermission, which might now drag on till the Second Coming?

My wife and daughter were the first to leave. Then my half-sister and Lenya left, and after them my mother, the dog, and me.

After we had been in the United States for a year, my father came. He settled in New Jersey. He plays bingo. Everything's normal. There is no applause to wait for, from anywhere.

My First Cousin

Life turned my first cousin into a criminal. It seems to me he was lucky. Otherwise, he would inevitably have become a high-ranking Party functionary.

This was due to a number of the most various preconditions. But I shouldn't jump ahead. . . .

His mother was my aunt Mara, the well-known literary editor. Her husband, Aron, was then the director of a military hospital. He also lectured and collected stamps. It was a good, close-knit family.

My cousin, though, had been born under rather curious circumstances. Before her marriage, my aunt had had a love affair with one of Party Secretary Kirov's deputies, Aleksandr Ugarov. Some old Leningraders still remember him.

He had a family, which he loved. But he also loved my

aunt. And eventually my aunt discovered that she was pregnant.

When it came time to give birth, she was taken to the hospital.

My mother went to Party Headquarters. She managed to get an appointment, and reminded Kirov's deputy about her sister and her problems.

Ugarov gloomily gave some orders. The flunkies of the Regional Party Office trooped to the maternity clinic with flowers and fruit. They also delivered to my aunt's lodgings a miniature inlaid card table, apparently requisitioned from nonproletarian class elements.

My aunt gave birth to a healthy, sweet little boy, who was named Boris. My mother decided to go to the Party Headquarters once again. This time she couldn't get an appointment, and not because Ugarov was suddenly putting on airs. Quite the contrary, in fact: Just a few days earlier the happy father had been arrested as an enemy of the people.

It was the year 1938. My aunt was left alone with the infant. It was a good thing that Ugarov hadn't been her husband. Otherwise my aunt would have been exiled. As it was, his wife and children were deported—which was also, of course, not very pleasant.

My aunt apparently knew how to handle herself. She was a handsome, energetic, and independent woman. If she was afraid of anything at all, it was the judgment of the Party.

Besides, Aron had come on the scene. It was obvious that he loved my aunt. He offered her his hand and heart. Aron was the son of a hat manufacturer, but he didn't look like the stereotype of a Jew, near-sighted and frail. He was a tall, strong, attractive man: a former radical student, a soldier in the Red Army, and a NEPman; later on, an administrative official; and, finally, in his declining years, a revisionist and dissident.

Aron idolized my aunt. Little Borya called him Papa.

The war began. We found ourselves in Novosibirsk. Borya was already three years old and in nursery school. I was a nursing infant.

Borya brought home some lumps of sugar for me. He carried them inside his cheek. At home he took them out and put them on a plate. I cried and refused to eat the sugar. In alarm, Borya said to his parents, "But the sugar's melting!"

Then the war ended and we no longer went hungry.

My cousin grew into a handsome adolescent of the Western European type. He had light eyes and dark, wavy hair. He looked like the young heroes of the progressive Italian cinema, in the opinion of our relatives.

He was an exemplary Soviet boy—a Pioneer, a top student, a soccer player, and a collector of scrap metal. He kept a notebook in which he wrote down wise sayings. He planted a birch tree in his courtyard. In the drama club he always played the Young Guard.

I was younger, but behaved worse; he was always being held up to me as an example. He was upright, modest, and well read. I was always being told, Borya does well in school, helps his parents, is good at sports. Borya won the school chemistry competition. Borya nursed a wounded nestling. Borya put together a detector receiver (to this day I have no idea what this is).

And suddenly something unreal happened. Something beyond description. I almost have no words.

To put it briefly, my cousin Borya pissed on the school director.

Borya was sitting in the Pioneer Room, working on the bulletin-board newspaper for Physical Culture Day. Around him was a crowd of schoolmates. Someone looking out the window said, "Here comes the Stoolie." The Stoolie was the nickname of the school director, Chebotaryov.

Whereupon, my cousin climbed up onto the windowsill, asked the girls to turn around, skillfully calculated his trajectory. And doused Chebotaryov from head to foot.

This was incredible and crazy. It was impossible to believe it. In a month several people who had been present doubted it had actually happened, so insane did the whole scene appear.

Director Chebotaryov's reaction was also highly unexpected. He completely lost his composure and suddenly began screaming in a rush of labor-camp slang, "I used to give it to the likes of you back in the camp! . . . I'll make you eat shit. . . . You son of a bacilli-laden bitch!"

The old prison taskmaster had awakened in Director Chebotaryov. And had it not been for this incident, who would ever have guessed his past? Always in a green felt hat, a Chinese cloak, always lugging a tightly stuffed, worn-out briefcase . . .

My first cousin performed this act one week before the end of school, thereby depriving himself of a gold medal. With difficulty, his parents persuaded the director to give Borya a certificate of completion.

I asked my cousin why he had done it. "I did what every student secretly dreams of doing," he replied. "When I saw the Stoolie that day, I realized it was now or never! I'll do it— or I'll stop respecting myself."

By that time I was already a rather malicious adolescent. I told my cousin, "In a hundred years they'll hang a memorial plaque on our school: 'Here Boris Dovlatov attended school—with all the ensuing consequences.'"

The family discussed my cousin's wild action for several months. Then Boris entered a theater institute. He had decided to become a drama specialist. People began to forget about his offense, especially since he did so brilliantly at school. He was the secretary of the Komsomol organization, a blood donor, the editor of the bulletin-board newspaper, and a goalie besides.

As he grew up, he became even handsomer. He looked even more like an Italian movie star. Girls pursued him with undisguised enthusiasm. Despite such attention, he was a chaste and shy young man. Feminine flirtatiousness sickened him. I remember one notation in his student notebook: "The main thing in a book and in a woman is not the form but the content."

Even now, after countless experiences and disappointments, this position seems to me a little boring. And now, as then, I only like beautiful women. I even have prejudices on this score. It seems to me, for example, that all fat women are liars. Especially if they have small breasts.

However, this story is not about me.

My cousin graduated from the theater institute, got his diploma with highest honors. An impeccable Komsomol dossier trailed after him: He worked on virgin-lands projects and commanded a construction unit; took an active part in a squad that assisted the police; was a terror to petit-bourgeois thinking and all vestiges of capitalism in the consciousness of the people.

He had the most honest eyes in the whole neighborhood.

He became a literary administrator; got a job in the Lenin Komsomol Theater. This was almost unbelievable. A very young man, just out of school, and such a position already!

As head of the literature department, he was demanding and businesslike. He fought on behalf of progressive art, and managed to do so with tact, restraint, and caution, while skillfully slipping the plays of Vampilov, Mrozek, Borschagovsky into production. Established Soviet playwrights were rather afraid of him. Rebellious young theater enthusiasts admired him.

He was sent on important business trips. He participated in a few Kremlin conferences. It was delicately suggested to him that he join the Party. He hesitated. It seemed to him he wasn't worthy.

And then, suddenly, my cousin once again distinguished himself. I don't know how to put it any better. Briefly, Borya committed twelve robberies.

He had a close friend named Tsapin, who worked for Intourist. And it came about that he and Tsapin managed a heist involving twelve tourist buses. They carried off suitcases, shortwave radios, tape recorders, umbrellas, raincoats, and hats. And a spare tire.

Twenty-four hours later they were arrested. We were in shock. My aunt ran to her friend Yuri Gherman. He telephoned his friends, among whom were generals in the militia.

My cousin was defended by the best lawyer in town, Kiselyov. In the course of the trial, certain fine points and details were brought to light. It turned out that the victims of the robbery were representatives of developing nations and members of progressive socialist organizations.

Kiselyov decided to make use of this. He asked my cousin, "Did you know that these people happened to be citizens of developing nations? As well as representatives of socialist organizations?"

"Unfortunately, no," Boris answered sensibly.

"Well, and if you had known? Would you still have attempted to encroach on their private possessions?"

My cousin's face expressed an extreme degree of hurt. The lawyer's question seemed to strike him as completely tactless. He raised his eyebrows in vexation, as if to signify, How can you ask? How can you even think it?

Kiselyov perked up noticeably. "And now, one last question," he said. "Wasn't it, rather, your belief that these gentlemen were representatives of reactionary strata of society?"

At this point the judge broke in. "Comrade Kiselyov, do not attempt to portray the accused as a fighter for world revolution."

But my cousin had managed to nod. Indicating, as it were, that such an assumption had flashed through his mind.

The judge raised his voice. "Let us confine ourselves to the facts the inquest has at its disposal."

Throughout the trial my cousin conducted himself bravely and without affectation. He smiled at the judge and bantered with him.

My cousin was given only three years. When the sentence was read, he didn't flinch. He was led away from the courtroom under guard.

Then there was an appeal, all kinds of solicitations, negotiations, and telephone calls. All useless.

My cousin was sent to Tiumen, a high-security labor

camp. We corresponded. All his letters began with the words "Things are normal here with me." Then there would be a list of requests, numerous but restrained and sober: "Two pairs wool socks . . . an English-language textbook . . . underwear . . . composition notebooks . . . a German-language textbook . . . garlic . . . lemons . . . a fountain pen . . . a French-language textbook . . . and also a manual for teaching yourself the guitar."

News from camp came through as entirely optimistic. The senior warden wrote my aunt, "Boris Dovlatov undeviatingly obeys all the injunctions of camp regulations . . . enjoys the respect of the other prisoners . . . systematically overfulfills his labor assignments . . . takes an active part in arranging cultural activities. . . ."

My cousin wrote that he had been appointed an orderly. Then a brigadier. And finally, chief administrator in charge of the bathhouse.

As a career, this was dizzying. And to be moving up in a labor camp was extraordinarily difficult. Equivalent advances outside jail would lead to the perquisites of a bureaucratic administration—to special shops, dachas, and travel abroad.

My cousin skyrocketed toward rehabilitation. He was the camp beacon. He was envied, he was admired. In a year's time he was transferred to chemistry. That is, to a free settlement, where he was assigned to work in a local chemical-industrial complex.

That was where he married. A self-sacrificing classmate named Liza went out to join him. She acted like the wife of a Decembrist. They became man and wife.

As for me during this time, I was kicked out of the university. Then I was drafted into the army. And I was assigned to serve as part of the military police—as a labor-camp guard.

So I was a guard. And Borya was a prisoner.

And it even came about that I stood guard over my cousin. True, not for very long. I don't really want to write about it. Otherwise everything would come out sounding overliterary, like Mikhail Sholokhov's *Tales from the Don*.

It's enough to say that I was a guard, and my cousin a prisoner.

We returned home at almost the same time. My cousin was released and I was demobilized. Our relatives arranged a grandiose banquet at the Metropole. First and foremost they were honoring my cousin, but now and then a good word was put in for me, too.

Our uncle Roman expressed himself like this: "There are people who remind you of reptiles. They live in swamps, and hide among the rocks. . . . And then there are people who remind you of mountain eagles. They soar higher than the sun, spreading their wings wide. . . . So let us drink to Borya, our mountain eagle! Let us wish that the clouds be left behind!"

"Bravo!" the relatives cried. "Our good boy, our eagle, our brave young warrior!"

In my uncle's speech I could detect motifs from Gorky's "Song of the Falcon."

Roman lowered his voice slightly and added, "Let's also drink to Seryozha, our eaglet! True, he's still young. His wings aren't so strong yet, but wide expanses wait for him, too!"

"God forbid!" my mother said rather loudly. My uncle gave her a reproachful look.

Once again my aunt made telephone calls to various people, and my cousin got a job at Lenfilm as something like a lighting assistant.

I began working for a factory newspaper, and started writing short stories on the side.

My cousin's career developed with gathering momentum. Soon he became a lab worker, then a dispatcher, then a senior dispatcher, and finally assistant to the director of a film. That is to say, he became someone of stature, with material responsibility.

It was no accident that in labor camp my cousin had moved so swiftly toward rehabilitation. Now it was clear he couldn't stop.

In a month, his photograph hung on the Board of Merit. He was loved by directors, by cameramen, and by the head of Lenfilm himself, Zvonaryov. More important, he was loved by the cleaning ladies.

He was promised a film of his own in the near future.

Sixteen old Communists at the studio were ready to recommend him for admission to the Party. But my cousin hesitated. He reminded me of Levin in *Anna Karenina*. On the eve of his marriage, Levin lamented that he had already lost his virginity in his youth. My cousin tormented himself with a similar problem. Namely, how was it possible to be a Communist with a criminal past?

The old Communists assured him that it was possible.

My cousin's accomplishments stood out all the more sharply against the pallid backdrop of my own. He was cheerful, dynamic, and laconic. He was sent on important business trips. Everyone foresaw a brilliant administrative career for him.

It was impossible to believe that he had been in prison.

People who knew us only slightly thought I was the one who had done time.

And then once again something happened, though not all at once. Strange lapses began to occur—as if the stately notes of the "Appassionata" were being wrecked by the shrill wails of a saxophone. My cousin pursued his career as before. Gave speeches at meetings. Went on business trips. But alongside this, he began to drink. And go after women, with unexpected enthusiasm.

He started to be seen in suspicious company. He was surrounded by drunkards and black marketeers. Whenever he was sober, he hurried to a meeting. After he had given a successful speech, he ran to meet his friends. In the beginning these paths didn't intersect.

There were times when he didn't show up at home for three days straight. He would disappear with some indecent woman. The majority of his women were unattractive. One of them, I remember, was named Greta. She had a goiter.

I said to my cousin, "You could do better than her."

"What are you, crazy?" he answered indignantly. "Don't you realize that she can get pure alcohol at work? And in unlimited quantities, at that?"

Evidently, my cousin was still governed by the doctrine of his youth: "In a woman and in a book the main thing is not the form, but the content."

Then my cousin beat up a waiter in the Narva restaurant. He had wanted the waiter to sing the Georgian love song "Suliko."

He began to be brought before the militia. Each time, the Party bureau at Lenfilm bailed him out, but each time less willingly. We waited to see how it would all end.

In the summertime he went off to Chita for the shooting of

a film called *Dauria*. And suddenly we learned that my cousin, driving an official car, had run over a man. What's more, an officer in the Soviet Army. Fatally.

This was a terrible time of suppositions and guesses. Information of the most contradictory kind kept coming in. It was said that Borya had been driving completely drunk. True, it was also said, that the officer had not been too sober either, though this had no significance, considering he was dead.

Everything was kept secret from my aunt. My uncles put together about four hundred rubles. I was supposed to fly to Chita, to learn all the details and to undertake some sensible actions: to arrange for packages to be forwarded, to hire a lawyer. "And, if possible, bribe the prosecuting attorney," Uncle Roman told me.

I started to get ready.

Late at night the telephone rang. I picked up the receiver. The calm voice of my cousin floated out of the silence: "Were you asleep?"

"Borya!" I shouted. "Are you alive? They're not going to shoot you? . . . Were you drunk?"

"I'm alive," my cousin answered. "They're not going to shoot me. And remember—it was an accident. I was driving—sober. They'll give me about four years, not more. Did you get the cigarettes?"

"What cigarettes?"

"Japanese. You see, Chita has a separate trade agreement with Japan. And they sell excellent cigarettes here called Hi-Lites. I sent you a carton for your birthday. Did you get them?"

"No. That's not important—"

"What do you mean, not important? They're first-class

cigarettes, manufactured under an American export license—"

But I interrupted him: "Are you in custody?"

"No," he said. "What for? I live in the hotel. The investigator comes to see me. Her name is Larissa. She's a nice plump girl—by the way, she sends her regards."

An unfamiliar female voice sang into the receiver: "Cuckoo, my little chickie!"

Then my cousin got on the line again. "It's absolutely useless for you to fly to Chita. The trial, I hope, will be in Leningrad. Does Mama know?"

"No," I said.

"There's going to be some racket. . . ."

"Borya!" I shouted. "What should I send you? You must be in a terrible state! After all, you've killed a man! Killed someone!"

"Don't shout! Officers are created in order to perish. And once again I repeat—it was an accident. The main thing is, where have those cigarettes gotten to?"

Soon people who had firsthand knowledge of the events arrived from Chita, and cleared up the details of the whole business.

Here's what happened:

It had been somebody's birthday, an outdoor celebration. Borya arrived late, toward evening, in an official car. As usual, there wasn't enough alcohol. The guests were getting a little depressed. The stores were shut.

Borya announced, "I'm going for moonshine. Anyone coming with me?"

He was tipsy. They tried to talk him out of it. In the end, three people went with him. This included the driver assigned to the car, who dozed in the backseat. Half an hour later, they knocked down a motorcyclist. He died instantly.

The members of the expedition became completely hysterical. My cousin, on the other hand, got very sober. He took precise and immediate action—namely, he still went to get the moonshine. This took fifteen minutes. Then he generously poured it out for the members of his expedition. Included was the slightly sobered official driver. He dozed off once again.

Only then did my cousin call the militia. A short time later, a police van pulled up. On arrival they found a corpse alongside a smashed motorcycle and four drunken persons, among whom my cousin appeared the most sober.

Lieutenant Dudko asked, "Which of you is the driver?" My cousin pointed to the sleeping driver. He was carried into the police van. The others gave their addresses and were taken to their separate lodgings.

My cousin hid out for three days, till the alcohol had worn off. Then he appeared at the police station and acknowledged his guilt.

By this time, quite naturally, the driver had sobered up. He was being held in a pretrial investigation cell. He was convinced that he had run over the man in a drunken stupor. Now my cousin appeared and declared that he had been at the wheel.

"Then why did you indicate Krachmalnikov Yuri Petrovich?" the lieutenant asked, growing angry.

"You asked who the driver was, so I told you."

"And where have you been for three days?"

"I got frightened—I was in shock. . . ." He tried to mimic the way someone with a fearful nature would act. The attempt rang false.

"Were you drunk while at the wheel?" the lieutenant asked.

"Not a bit," my cousin answered.

"That I doubt."

However, it was already impossible to prove anything one way or the other. The members of the expedition swore that Borya hadn't been drinking. The driver escaped with a professional reprimand.

My cousin had acted cunningly. Now he would have to be tried not as a drunken driver but as someone who had caused an accident. The female investigator, Larissa, said to him, "Even in bed you continue to lead the investigation astray."

A week later he showed up in Leningrad.

My aunt already knew everything. She didn't carry on. She made telephone calls to writers who had connections with the militia. To Yuri Gherman, as always, to Metter, Saparov . . . As a result, my cousin was left in peace until the trial. All he was asked to do was sign a pledge that he wouldn't leave town.

On one of his first days home, my cousin dropped in to see me. He asked, "You did guard duty near Leningrad, didn't you? Do you know the local system of labor camps?"

"More or less. I was in Obukhovo, Gorelyov, at Piskarovka. . . ."

"Which one do you think would be best for me to be in?"

"Obukhovo, I think. The security is not as tight."

"Then I'd better go there and look around."

We went to Obukhovo. We stopped by the barracks, had a talk with the orderly, found out who was there of the reenlisted men I would know. After a moment Sergeants Goderidze and Osipenko came running into the barracks.

We embraced. I introduced them to my cousin. Then I

asked who was still there of the old prison-camp administration.

"Captain Deryabin," the soldiers answered.

Captain Deryabin I remembered well. He was a comparatively good-hearted, harmless lush. The prisoners used to sneak off with his cigarettes. At the time that I was doing my service, Deryabin had been a lieutenant.

We telephoned into the camp. In a minute Deryabin appeared at the guardhouse.

"Ah!" he cried. "Seryoga's showed up! Let's have a look at you and see how you turned out. I heard you went and became a writer. Here, write up this incident from life. One of my prisoners catapulted himself out of an exterior work zone. I had brought a brigade of these zeks out of the camp on sanitation duty. I left the convoy. Went off to have a quick one. I come back—one zek is missing. He'd flown off! They bent down a pine tree, see, and buckled the guy to the top branch with a rigging belt. Then let go. And then in midflight the zek unbuckles himself, and it's good-bye! He flies just short of the railway crossing. However, it turns out he was just a little off in his reckoning. He was hoping to land in the snow by the sawmill. But it turns out he bangs down in the yard of the Regional Military Committee. And there's also this detail, pure literature: When they grabbed him, he bit the commanding officer on the nose."

I introduced Deryabin to my cousin.

"Call me Lyokha," Captain Deryabin said, holding out his hand.

"Bob."

"So what do you think?" I said. "It wouldn't be bad to go have a little nip ourselves." We decided to leave the barracks and go to the nearest wooded area. We invited Goderidze and

Osipenko. Got four bottles of booze out of a briefcase, sat down on a fallen spruce.

"Well, best of luck!" the prison guards said.

Five minutes later, my cousin was embracing Deryabin. And meanwhile he kept asking him questions. "How's the heating? Are there many dogs on guard? Do they use a lot of solitary confinement here?"

"You'll be all right here," the soldiers assured him.

"A good camp," Goderidze kept repeating. "You'll get your health back, rest up, look like a weight lifter. . . ."

"And there's a store right nearby," Osipenko put in, "just beyond the railroad crossing. White wine, red, beer . . ."

In half an hour Deryabin was saying, "Get yourselves jailed, boys, while I'm still around. Because they're going to retire Lyokha Deryabin, and then you'll regret it. . . . Then the troubles will begin. Then you'll be in for it. Creeps will come, dropouts from higher education. . . . Then you'll think of Lyokha Deryabin."

Borya jotted down Deryabin's home telephone number.

"And I'll write down yours," said Deryabin.

"No sense in that," my cousin answered. "I'll be here in two weeks."

In the train going home he said, "So far, things don't look too bad." I almost burst into tears. Apparently the booze was having its effect on me.

Soon the trial began. My cousin was again defended by Kiselyov. The public was continually breaking into applause for him.

Curiously enough, the victim of the events, as Kiselyov portrayed them, was not the deceased man, Korobchenko, but my cousin. In his concluding speech, the lawyer said, "A human life reminds one of a mountain road with many dangerous turns. One of these proved to be fatal for the defendant. . . ."

My cousin was given three years. But this time in a maximum-security labor camp.

The day of the trial I received a package from Chita. It contained ten packages of Japanese cigarettes—Hi-Lites.

Borya was sent to Obukhovo. He wrote me that the camp was a good one, and the camp administration fairly humane. Captain Deryabin proved to be a man of his word. He assigned Borya the job of bread slicer. This was a privileged and much-envied position.

Meanwhile, my cousin's wife, Liza, had given birth to a little girl named Natasha. One day she called me and said, "We've been granted a group visit with Borya. If you're free, let's go together. It will be hard for me to go alone with the baby."

Four of us went—my aunt, Liza, two-month-old Natasha, and I. It was a hot August day. Natasha cried the whole way there. Liza was nervous. My aunt got a headache.

We pulled up to the guardhouse and found the Visiting Room. Besides us, there were six other visitors. The prisoners were separated from us by a glass barrier.

Liza unswaddled the baby. My cousin still hadn't appeared. I went over to the reenlistee on duty.

"And where is Dovlatov?" I asked.

"Sit down and wait," he answered.

I said, "Telephone the orderly and call out my cousin. And tell Lyokha Deryabin that I said to have you disciplined."

The guard on duty changed his tone. "I don't take orders from Deryabin. I take orders from the intelligence officer."

"Go on," I said. "Telephone."

Just then my cousin appeared. He was wearing a gray prison outfit. His hair, shaved close, had grown to a crew cut. He was tanned and his body seemed longer.

My aunt pushed a package of apples, sausage, and chocolate to him through the opening in the glass barrier.

Liza said to her little daughter, "Tatusya, this is Papa. See, this is Papa!"

But my cousin kept looking at me. Then he said, "You're wearing revolting trousers. And they're such an awful shit color. How about if I put you in touch with a tailor here? There's a Jew in the zone here who sews incredible pants. Not only is he a *portnoy* by trade, but his name is Portnoy. Some coincidence, right?"

I yelled, "What are you talking about? What difference does it make what I'm wearing?"

"Don't worry," he said. "It won't cost you a thing. I'll lay out the money, you'll buy the material, and he'll sew you the pants. The Jew says, 'The backside is the face of a man.' And just look at yours, all those creases."

It seemed to me that for a repeat offender he was acting excessively fastidious.

"The money," my aunt said, suddenly tense, "where does it come from? I know that in labor camp you're not supposed to have money."

"Money is like microbes," Borya said. "It's everywhere. When we achieve true communism it will all be different."

"At least take a look at your daughter," Liza begged.

"I saw," my cousin said. "A fine little girl."

I said, "How's the food?"

"Pretty bad. Though, it's true, I don't eat in the mess hall.

93

We send one of the reenlistees out to the food store. But it often happens that you can't get a thing there. After one o'clock it's too late to get sausage or eggs. . . . Yes, Nikita really messed up agriculture. And to think there was a time when we fed all of Europe. Our one hope is the private sector. The restoration of NEP—"

"Not so loud," my aunt said.

My cousin beckoned to the guard on duty to come over and said something to him in a low voice. The guard started making excuses. We could catch only fragments of sentences.

"Look, I asked you to get it by twelve-thirty," my cousin said.

"I remember," the guard told him. "Don't worry. Tolik will be back in ten minutes."

"Dima, I'll get insulted. . . ."

"Borya, you know the kind of man I am: if I promise something, that means I'll do it. Tolik will be back in literally five minutes."

"But my cousin wants a drink right now."

I asked, "What's going on?"

My cousin answered, "He sent some ace out to get vodka, and that was the end of him. . . . It's a real bordello around here, no military discipline at all."

"They'll put you in solitary confinement," Liza said.

"So? You think there are no human beings around solitary?"

The child started crying again. Liza took offense. My cousin seemed unattentive and indifferent to her. My aunt kept taking one medicine after another.

Visiting time was running out. One of the zeks was led away almost by force. He kept trying to tear himself away and

94

then yelled out, "Nadka, if you fuck around, I'll kill you. I'll hunt you down and cripple you like a monkey—this I guarantee. And remember, you bitch, Vovik loves you!"

"Time to go," I said. "Time's up."

My aunt turned away. Liza rocked the baby.

"And the vodka?" my cousin asked.

"You'll drink it yourself."

"I wanted to drink it with you."

"It's not worth it, brother. This isn't much of a place for drinking."

"Well, you would know. But that guard, I'll let him have it, all the same. For me the main thing in a person is reliability."

Suddenly Tolik appeared with a bottle. You could tell that he had been hurrying to get there. "Here it is," he said. "A ruble thirty change."

"Do it so that I don't see anything, fellas," the guard on duty said, handing Borya an enameled mug.

My cousin filled it quickly. Everyone took a swallow—the zeks, their relatives, the guards, the soldiers, the guard on duty himself.

Lifting the mug, one unshaven, tattooed zek said, "To our mighty Motherland! To Comrade Stalin personally! To our victory over fascist Germany! Let's hear it for the surface missiles—ba-boom! . . ."

"Long live the reactionary clique of Imre Nagy!" another zek said, seconding him.

The guard on duty touched my cousin on the shoulder. "Bob, I'm sorry, your time is up."

We said good-bye. I shook my cousin's hand through the barrier. My aunt looked at her son in silence. Liza suddenly burst into tears, waking up Natasha, who had just fallen asleep. She started to yell.

We walked out and began looking for a taxi.

About a year went by. My cousin wrote that everything was going well. He worked as a bread slicer, and when Deryabin retired, Borya became an electrical repairman.

Then a representative of the Internal Affairs Administration got in touch with my cousin. They had decided to have a documentary film made about labor camps, to show that Soviet camps were the most humane in the world. The film was intended for internal consumption. It was entitled, dryly, "Methods of Detainment in Maximum-Security Labor Colonies."

My cousin traveled around to distant prison camps for locations. A government car was put at his disposal. He was consigned all the appropriate equipment. Two escorts would invariably accompany him—Goderidze and Osipenko.

My cousin often managed to make short visits home. He visited me a few times.

By summer the film was ready. My cousin had been cameraman, director, and narrator, all at the same time. A preview was arranged, with generals and colonels in the audience. At the panel evaluation afterward, General Shurepov said, "A good, much-needed film . . . As pleasant to watch as *A Thousand and One Nights* . . ." Borya got a lot of praise.

I finally understood the ruling trait in my cousin's character: he was a natural-born existentialist. He could act only in extreme situations: build a career only in prison, fight for life only on the edge of the abyss.

Finally, that fall, he was released. What follows will sound familiar. My aunt telephoned Yuri Gherman. My cousin was hired as an unskilled workman at a documentary-film studio. Two months later he was working as a sound technician. And in another half year he was head of the department of acquisitions.

Just about the same time, I was laid off from work, this time for good. I wrote short stories and lived off my mother's pension.

When my aunt fell ill and died, a portrait of a gray-eyed, handsome man was found in her papers. This was Kirov's deputy Aleksandr Ivanovich Ugarov. He looked like my cousin, though a considerably younger version of him. Even before this, Borya had known who his father was. From then on everyone spoke openly about it.

My cousin could have attempted to get in touch with his relatives. But he didn't want to. He said to me, "I have you, and no one else."

Then he thought a moment and added, "How strange! Both of us with Armenian mothers, and I'm half Russian, you're half Jewish. But we both like vodka with beer."

In 1978 I decided to emigrate. My cousin could have applied, too, but he said he wouldn't go.

He had once again begun to drink and get into fights in restaurants. He was threatened with being laid off from work. It was as though he could live only in confinement. When he was out of prison, he let himself go and even got sick.

I said to him one last time, "Let's both go."

He reacted listlessly and sadly. "The whole business isn't for me. You have to take all those official steps. . . . You have to assure everyone that you're Jewish. I'd find it embarrassing. If only it was one-two-three, in the middle of a hangover, and there you are in Rome, right on Capitoline Hill."

At the airport my cousin cried. I could see how he had aged. Besides which, it's always harder to stay than to leave.

For four years now, I've lived in New York, and for four years I've been sending packages to Leningrad. And suddenly one arrived from there.

I opened it in the post office. In it lay a blue knit sweatshirt with an emblem of the Olympic Games. And a heavy metal corkscrew of the latest model, with greetings from Boris.

I thought to myself, What were the most precious things I ever got in my life? And I realized: four pieces of lump sugar, Japanese cigarettes called Hi-Lites, and now this corkscrew.

I covered my face with my hands. I understood that I was alone.

Glasha

With each passing year she looked more like a human being. (I can't say as much for most of my friends.) I felt embarrassed changing my clothes in front of her.

My friend Sevostyanov used to say, "She's the only normal member of your family."

I first brought her home on the palm of my hand, a month-old fox terrier puppy named Glasha. Her coloring was like birchbark, her nose like a tiny boxer's glove. In a word, she was irresistible.

Until she was roughly a year old, she seemed like an ordinary dog. Chewed our shoes. Begged for scraps. We trained her quite carelessly, fed her whatever was around, and walked her morning and evening for about ten minutes.

There was none of your "Give me your paw," none of your

"Sit up!" or "Roll over." But then, we had long conversations with her, my mother, my wife, and I, and later on, when she was old enough to converse, my daughter.

Glasha was going on thirteen months when a certain Lyosha Bobrov appeared. He and I had been students together in the philology department of the university. They expelled me, whereas Lyosha graduated successfully.

He was an entirely healthy, even aggressive, young fellow. He chased after girls, led a scandalous life, got drunk. Then he got married. He used to call his wife by an English word, "Filly."

He went to work for Intourist for a year, at which point he was overtaken by extreme pessimism. That was when Bobrov took a job as game warden in the Podporozhski region. He began a life in the woods like Henry David Thoreau. He hunted, pickled his own mushrooms, and made intensive use of his own home still.

From time to time he would show up in Leningrad. Once, he dropped by unexpectedly, saw my dog, and said, "What have you got here? She's a dog bred to dig a fox out of its burrow, and you've turned her into a house pet. Why don't you let me take her back to the preserve and teach her how to hunt? Then in two months I'll bring her back to you."

We thought about it. After all, why not? A dog should be allowed to develop its natural instincts.

Two months went by, then three, then four. Bobrov did not show up. I wrote to him. No answer. My mother kept saying, "It's boring without Glasha here. There's nobody to talk to."

My daughter cried. Finally my wife said to me, "Go bring the dog home."

Our friend Valeri Grubin decided to accompany me. Our train got to Podporozhye by seven in the evening. It was thirteen kilometers to the hunting preserve of Rovskoe. No transportation of any kind was available. There wasn't even a road; you had to go along the frozen Svir' River. What was to be done?

A local lush advised us to hire a sled for the price of a bottle, which we did. Two teenage boys agreed to take us there. We traveled the whole way in silence. The mare took slow and cautious steps on the ice. Our attempts at conversation with these country kids met with no success. Finally the horse stopped.

"On that hill, there, is Rovskoe," they said.

We settled with them and started the climb up the hill. It was completely dark. No light anywhere, no sound. We went along, guessing our way by the river. Suddenly Grubin disappeared. I screamed, "Where are you?"

In response, a sepulchral voice said, "Here . . . I've fallen down an abandoned well."

I groped my way to the sound. I came upon a square black hole, lay down on the snow, and carefully looked over the edge.

In the depths of the pit a light glimmered. Grubin was lighting a cigarette. "It's damp down here," he complained.

I crawled backward, chose a three-meter-long sapling, worked on it for about an hour. Finally, with the help of a pocketknife, I managed to make a pole. I pulled my friend up to the surface. Grubin thanked me and said, "Wait, lower me back down. I forgot my matches."

We got to Rovskoe only by daylight. It turned out the boys had left us off more than four kilometers from our destination.

Lyosha Bobrov stood on his doorstep, smiling in embarrassment. With a howl, Glasha threw herself at me. She was shaggy all over, and thin.

"Chilled to the bone?" Bobrov asked. "Want a drink?"

No matter how furious a Russian may be, offer him a drink and his mood immediately improves.

At the table Bobrov said to me, "I was in Leningrad twice. I wanted to bring the dog back, but I couldn't. I've gotten used to her."

We learned that Glasha had performed heroic feats. First of all, she had saved a puppy from drowning by dragging it out of a pool of water. Also, she had been the first one to catch the scent of a bear on the prowl. Finally, she had strangled a fox.

It bothered me that Glasha had killed a living creature. But what could you do? That was her instinct.

Grubin reminded me of an adventure we had once had. We had been eating together in the Baltic restaurant and had started a conversation with our waitress. We even invited her to share a bottle of cognac with us, and it was all done in a friendly way, without any ulterior motive. But then she added an extra six rubles to our bill. I got very angry, not about the money, of course—I was upset someone would act that way. Grubin kept saying, "What are you so surprised about? If a nightingale sings, it's not out of happiness: he can't help it, it's his instinct. A nightingale sings, a waitress cheats. She just can't help it."

"Sell the dog," Bobrov said.

"What! You must be crazy!"

"All right, then give her to me as a present. She'll be better off here."

"Maybe she will, but what about us?"

We drank a little more and then went to get some sleep. We woke up around dinnertime. There were four men we didn't know in the dining room. Bobrov took me aside and said, "They're KGB. Tomorrow they go off elk hunting."

"What the hell do they need elk for?" I said. "Don't they have enough of us to go after?"

"No, they're all right," Bobrov whispered. "After work they change."

"Oh? Who do they go after then?"

These guys from the State Security Organs had a look of power to them. They had something in common, all were very familiar types: standard smooth faces, neat parts in their hair, wool clothing.

One came up to me. He started asking questions in an abrupt, precise way. "Your dog? . . . Good . . . What's her name? Glasha? How long since she's been in heat? You don't know? And who is supposed to know? Her ears are free of pus? Yes? Excellent . . ."

"Sit down and have something to eat," Bobrov told everyone.

We had a leisurely meal together. The KGB guys got out some vodka. The subject matter of the conversation kept getting ticklish, though.

"Freedom?" one said. "You just give a Russian freedom. The first thing he'll go and do is slit his mother-in-law's throat!"

I asked, "Why did they put Misha Haifetz in jail? Other people publish abroad, and nothing happens. And Haifetz hasn't even published his work, by the way."

"And too bad for him he didn't," another of them said. "If he had, they wouldn't have jailed him. This way, who needs him?"

"Sakharov reasons like a child," another said. "His ideas are useless. What is all this nonsense about human rights? A Russian needs only one right: the right to get over his hangover!"

"It's time we were going," I said. "Thank you."

We got our things together. Bobrov said good-bye to Glasha. His wife, Filly (I've forgotten her real name), even wept quietly.

We went out onto the road. The KGB crew came out onto the porch. "Come and visit," one said. "We've got a terrific museum. Not for the general public, of course, but I can arrange it. You have my address and telephone number."

"And you come by, too," I said.

"But only with a warrant," Grubin said.

The secret policeman gave him a close look and then said, "A warrant is not a problem."

We said good-bye and made our way back along the river. Glasha ran beside me without looking back.

"I wonder what they have in that museum of theirs," I said.

"God knows," Grubin said. "Maybe Bukharin's finger-nails."

About two years later I moved to Tallinn without my family. Glasha went with me. Shortly after we arrived, she accomplished her next great feat.

The newspaper I worked for sent me off on assignment to an island, so I had to leave the dog with friends while I was away. These friends happened to live in an apartment that was heated by a coal stove. While Glasha was there, they lit the stove one evening when someone had accidentally closed the flue. Everybody went to sleep.

Charcoal fumes began to fill the apartment. Nobody woke up except Glasha, who took a rational course of action. She went to the bed of the master of the house and dragged the blanket off him. The master of the house threw a slipper at her and pulled the blanket back up. Glasha dragged it off again, and this time started barking. Finally the bipeds in the house began to realize what was going on. They flung open the door and ran out into the street. The master of the house fell into a snowdrift. Glasha staggered about and kept vomiting for quite a long time.

That day my friends brought her four hundred grams of tenderloin, straight from the cafeteria of the Central Committee. This was a unique occurrence, possibly the first time in the history of the Party that exclusive privileges were awarded to someone worthy of them.

It was in Tallinn that I first began to think about finding a husband for Glasha. I called up a cinematographer I knew, and he gave me a few addresses and telephone numbers.

My dog's aristocratic pedigree required me to be very fussy. I decided on a male dog named Rezo. The Georgian name promised physical strength and stormy emotions. Added to that, Rezo's owner, a pretty woman named Anechka Pai, turned out to be a journalist on the Estonian-language newspaper that was our counterpart.

The love act was supposed to take place in a vacant lot by the hippodrome. Rezo looked beautiful. He was a reddish, brawny fellow with insolent eyes. He vibrated nervously and whimpered softly.

Anya had come dressed in a short sheepskin coat and patent-leather boots. She was full of admiration for my dog. She exclaimed, "What a darling!" adding, "Only, very skinny," as if she doubted her household would benefit from such a daughter-in-law.

"It's the style these days," I said. Anya pointed to her own plump rib cage in a gesture of doubt.

We exchanged documents. Glasha's pedigree was a sight

more impressive than the genealogy of my aristocrat friend Volodya Trubetskoy. Rezo's papers also turned out to be very proper.

"Well, then, here goes," Anya said with a sigh, and she let Rezo off his leash. I also let go of Glasha.

It was a sunny, early winter afternoon. Rosy shadows lay on the snow. Once he sensed his freedom, Rezo went slightly crazy. He began to race around, barking, doing laps in three widening circles. Glasha observed him with slack interest.

After all that running, Rezo toppled over into the snow. Evidently he wanted to cool his ardor, or else show us what lengths he would go to in order to avoid reckless action.

Then he shook himself off and ran toward us. Glasha became tense and lifted her tail. The male eyed her ravenously and walked around her several times. Glasha's tail shuddered invitingly. She walked up to Rezo and brushed against his shoulder.

Then the unexpected happened. Yelping shrilly, the young male tore past us. He reached his mistress and snuggled up against her patent-leather boots.

Glasha turned away in disgust. Rezo trembled and made little whimpering noises.

"So, what's the matter with you? What's the matter?" Anya said, trying to soothe him. "Come on, be a man!"

But Rezo only whined and trembled. He was a high-spirited impotent, that insolent Rezo, a type often encountered among middle-aged males of the Caucasus.

Anya was embarrassed for her charge. She even seemed to want to compensate me, somehow, for his failure. As she said good-bye, she whispered, "Kalyu is flying off to Minsk for a seminar. I'll call you at the end of the week."

Anya really did telephone, but my rough-mannered friend Tatyana cursed her rather badly. Then, when the newspaper fired me, Anya volunteered to write a piece about me for her Estonian newspaper. She even thought up a title: "Seen Through Dark Glasses," to suggest that I darkened and debunked every subject I wrote about. A friend of mine who was an instructor on the Central Committee managed to block its publication, but not without some effort.

But let's get back to my dog. Three times or so I tried to marry her off. All three times were flops. The second bridegroom possessed plebeian leanness and strength. He reminded me of a gym teacher from the provinces. He decided not to waste time and dispensed with all amorous foreplay. Decided to steamroll her, as they say. Glasha responded with a nasty bite. But he kept right on going after her, like a true meathead. He was a real happy type, with no complexes whatsoever.

So why did he turn Glasha off? It's apparent here that even a dog can't do without that drop of romance. . . .

The third suitor scratched himself without stop. On top of that, he had a weak bladder, and his coat was sort of dingy, with little bald patches. But his pedigree, which I looked up, was truly extraordinary. Obviously a degenerate. Just like Volodya Trubetskoy.

Glasha simply ignored him; and so she remained a virgin. Later on, it was too late. My cinematographer friend said, "What if she suddenly couldn't manage to give birth, what then? We have the right to risk our own lives, but to risk someone else's life is something decent people don't do."

So Glasha remained a maiden. How many are around today? They say it's easier to meet a spy than one of those.

On the spiritual plane, though, her life worked out unusually well. Glasha was acquainted with Yevgeny Yevtushenko, Vasily Aksyonov, Anatoly Naiman, Yevgeny Rein. She sat on Daniil Granin's lap and Vera Panova's, ate from the hands of Akhmatova and Kornei Chukovsky, tore the trousers of the esteemed critic Efim Etkind.

I visited Joseph Brodsky with her. Delighted with my punctuality, he said, "You came at exactly two—that's normal. But how did Glasha manage to be so punctual?"

She was surrounded by esoteric poets, Suprematist painters, composers of atonal music, and sculptors of nonrepresentational constructions. All of them were indefatigable critics of the regime, especially when in their cups. With friends like that, she could hardly have turned out politically loyal. Actually, she herself behaved no better. To be specific, she barked at policemen and generally hated all uniforms, whether on soldiers, sailors, or ticket collectors. Along with this, her displeasure was aroused by red banners and billboards bearing revolutionary slogans, and to top it off, she liked to relieve herself behind a certain building, at the base of a four-meter-tall portrait of Brezhnev.

In short, Glasha was a born nonconformist, which meant for her, as for me, future emigration. This is exactly what came about in 1978. After I was forced to make the banal choice between prison and America, Glasha landed with me and my mother in the West.

The main thing that struck her about New York City was the vast quantity of squirrels. I thought it would be all those conversations at home with her about crime in America, how people were being robbed and murdered all around you, how it was frightening to go outside. Nevertheless, the squirrels kept jumping across the lawns. If one of them had shown up in Moscow, there would be five hundred people running after it to see. But I'm getting away from my subject.

Alas, Glasha did not become an American. What is the main quality of Americans? I immediately decided it was their optimism. In the courtyard of our building there was a man who got around in a wheelchair. If you asked him, "How are things?" he answered, "Fine," without the slightest trace of self-consciousness. Or else you saw a girl on the street, pale, disheveled, heavy-legged, wearing a T-shirt that said, "I'm Ursula Andress." Again, not the least bit self-conscious. And so on.

My dog had a different psychological makeup. If there were any optimistic aspects in Glasha's nature, I never noticed them. She didn't even wag her tail very often. If a stranger moved to pet her, she snarled.

She somehow walked sideways. She looked at those around her as though she were challenging them to a duel. If she encountered a big, well-groomed borzoi on the street, she would give out a contemptuous, "N-af-f!"

In brief, Glasha had little talent for democracy. She was short on kindheartedness and loaded with neuroses. The sexual revolution never touched her. A typical middle-aged woman émigré from Russia.

As for the rest, I'll get it down quickly, in outline form. Soon Glasha got old and began ailing. She started getting convulsions more and more often. Her legs kept giving out.

We took her to a vet. My Americanized daughter, Katya— she had arrived in the States well ahead of me, and was just finishing high school—consulted with the vet in English. I asked her in Russian, "Well, what does he say?"

109

Katya said, "It's her age. And also—I don't know how to translate this—in general, she has some female problem. She absolutely must have an operation."

"How long will it prolong her life? Ask him."

"What's the difference? What if it's only one day?"

"I heard something about a thousand dollars."

"So who the hell cares about that?"

I looked at my daughter with interest. Up until that moment, she had seemed like a typical American girl— happy and carefree, with a dollop of pragmatism. And now, suddenly, such a stand.

Actually, what do we know about typical Americans?

Glasha died two months after the operation. She went to sleep and never woke up. It was lucky she went like that. Who do I thank?

We lived without a dog for close to a year. Then we bought a month-old dachshund in a pet store. We named him Yashka.

Yashka's legs are crooked. He has a chest like Arnold Schwarzenegger's. And he's as lively as quicksilver.

Once, our designer friend Mikhnovich dropped by for a visit. He hugged Yashka for a long time. Then he gave his opinion: "Good material."

Yashka has no neuroses whatsoever. He's always in a great mood. His bent for democracy verges on total lack of discrimination. He greets every guest with a happy bark. Every bitch in the neighborhood gets his leering attention, especially the tall, aristocratic borzois.

"And him with his appearance!" my wife says.

My mother keeps saying, sadly, "The worst thing is, I'm getting to like this one. It's not fair to Glasha, but what can I do?"

The Colonel Says
I Love You

"Our world is absurd," I say to my wife, "and a man's enemies are the people in his own house."

My wife takes offense, though I say this as a joke. She comes back with, "I'll tell you who your enemies are: cheap port and bleached blondes!"

"Which means," I say, "that I am a true Christian, for Christ taught us to love our enemies."

Such conversations have been going on for twenty years, give or take a few weeks.

I emigrated to America dreaming of divorce. The sole ground for divorce was my wife's extreme imperturbability. Her serenity had no limits. It is remarkable how two opposite qualities, serenity and contrariness, can coexist in one person.

We met in 1963. This is how it happened:

I had a room in a communal apartment, but a room with

its own entrance. The window faced a garbage dump. My friends got together practically every evening at my place.

Once, I woke up in the middle of the night. Saw the dirty dishes on the table and an overturned chair. Remembered the evening that had just been, with a stab. Some of us had gone out to buy more vodka three times. Someone had actually said, "Let's go get something to eat at Yeliseyev's! It's three blocks there, and about the same distance back."

I started thinking about what breakfast would be like in a messy room.

Suddenly I sensed that I was not alone. Someone was sleeping on the couch between the refrigerator and the record player. There were rustlings and sighs. I asked, "Who's there?"

"Suppose it's Lena," a calm female voice answered unexpectedly.

I got to thinking. You don't hear the name Lena so very often. In my circle of friends, Tamaras and Larissas predominated. I asked, "What's your status, Lena? To put it more simply, who is your *socius qua non?*"

There was a pause. Then the calm female voice said, "Gurevich forgot me."

Gurevich was someone I knew through buying books on the black market. He was arrested two years later.

"What do you mean, forgot?"

"Gurevich got drunk and took a taxi home."

I began to remember something. "You were wearing a brown dress?"

"Basically. Green, actually. Gurevich tore it. But I slept in somebody's work shirt."

"That's my old army work shirt. A relic, so to speak. When you leave, please take it off."

"There's some kind of medal here in front. . . ."

"That," I said, "is a sports pin."

"So sharp—it kept me up all night."

"Who could blame it?" I said. Finally I remembered who she was. Slim, pale, with Mongolian eyes.

By this time it was getting light.

"Look the other way," Lena said.

I covered my face with a newspaper. Instantly the acoustics changed. The young lady proceeded to walk to the door—to judge by the sound, in my velveteen slippers. I crawled out from under the blanket. The day had begun in a very strange way.

Then some awkward maneuvering in the hall. A towel around my not-so-bony rib cage. The army shirt that didn't quite reach her knees. We got past each other with some difficulty. I headed for the shower. After a shower, a relative degree of lucidity always enters my life. I came out after three minutes to find the table set with coffee, cookies, jam. Also fish in aspic, for some reason.

By this time, Lena had put on her dress. The classic rip by the collar—the mark of Fima Gurevich's unbridled sensuality—became her well.

"Truly," I said, "it *is* green."

We had breakfast, making small talk. It was all amiable, easy, and even pleasant, like a kind of corrective to the general craziness of the situation.

Lena got her things together, put on her shoes, and said, "I'm off."

"Thank you for a most pleasant morning."

Suddenly I heard her say, "I'll be here around six."

"Good," I said.

I thought of the time I was leaving a bathhouse with a friend when a policeman stopped us. We both got very tense and asked, "What's going on?"

And he said, "You wouldn't happen to remember when Akhmatova's *Rosary* was published?"

My friend said, "Nineteen-fourteen, Hyperborean Press, Saint Petersburg."

The policeman said, "Thank you. You can go."

"Where?" we asked.

"Wherever you wish," he answered. "You are free."

At the time, I had been struck by the mixture of the everyday and the absurd. And now I had a similar impression from Lena's "I'll be here around six."

And I had an appointment at five-thirty. To make matters worse, it wasn't with a woman, but with Brodsky. After that, there was supposed to be a dinner celebrating someone's successful thesis defense.

I called to cancel the appointment. The dinner I ignored. I rushed home from work in a taxi. I found myself thinking, I should have ordered another set of keys.

I waited. She arrived close to six. She opened a string shopping bag and unpacked cans of food, eggs, and hake. "You do whatever you have to do," she said, "and I'll get all this ready."

Suddenly I had a wild thought: maybe she's got me mixed up with somebody else? With some dear and close person? Maybe the world has really gone mad?

We ate supper. I sat down to work. Lena washed the dishes and turned on the television. My television had not worked in two years. And now it suddenly started working, just like new.

I began to notice a few small changes. Some foreign jars had appeared above the sink. Something suede hung in my closet. A pair of short beige boots stood by the refrigerator. Even the scent of the air in the apartment was different.

It grew late. Lena asked, "Would you like tea or coffee?"

"Tea." We drank tea with some kind of gingerbread cookies. I hadn't eaten gingerbread for about thirty years.

Suddenly I noticed that it was one in the morning. Time to go to sleep, it would seem. Lena said, "Go sit in the kitchen for a moment."

I sat there, smoked. Read last Tuesday's paper. When I went into the other room, she was asleep. On the very same couch. Only instead of the army shirt, I saw something pink.

I lay down on my bed and listened: not a sound. Not even the smallest flirtatious rustle in her sleep. I waited for about ten minutes and also fell asleep.

In the morning, everything went just as before. The slight awkwardness, a shower, coffee with milk . . .

"This time," she said, "I'll be delayed. I'll be here after eleven. So don't worry."

I went off to the editorial office, from there to the Union of Soviet Journalists' bar. I met a Swedish woman who invited me to her hotel. She kept saying, "Cossack, pour me some of that Russian vodka!"

My friends were planning to go to an underground concert, to hear a certain avant-garde musician, and a highly unusual one, you might say: he played the cello lying down. In a word, temptations by the carload. But I hurried home. I was late getting back to my madhouse.

When she arrived that evening, I said, "Lena, let's have a talk. It seems to me we have to get some things out in the open. Something strange is going on. I have to ask a few ticklish questions. Do you mind if I ask them straight out?"

"Go on," she said. And her face was as untroubled as a dam.

I asked, "You have no place to live, right?"

The young lady got slightly offended. More precisely, she showed some surprise. "Why do you say that? I have an apartment on Dachny Prospect. Why do you ask?"

"Well, no reason, really— It seemed to me . . . I thought . . . Then just one more question. Completely between friends—a thousand times pardon—are you perhaps attracted to me?"

There was a pause. I felt myself blushing. Finally she said, "I don't make claims on you." That was how she put it— claims, she says, I don't make.

Then a pause that was even more tense than before—for me. She was full of serenity, the look in her eyes as cold and firm as the corner of a suitcase.

Here I got to thinking. Perhaps her serenity put her above making sexual distinctions? Above feeling any biological pull toward a man? Even above the idea of a permanent place of residence?

"And now, one last question. Only don't get mad. And if I'm wrong, just forget I ever said this. To make it short, there's just one more possibility. . . . You wouldn't by any chance be employed by the KGB?"

Anything is possible, I thought. I was, after all, somewhat known, in thought and behavior unrestrained. I drank rather a lot. Shot my mouth off. My name had been mentioned on Russian broadcasts from West German radio. Maybe they thought I was a budding dissident, and had assigned this unbelievable woman to me?

Now, I thought, she's really got to start yelling. If I'm wrong, she'll raise the roof, and if I'm right, she'll raise it even more.

I heard her say, "No. I work in a beauty parlor." And then, "If you don't have any more questions, let's have some tea."

That was how everything began. During the day, I would run around looking for hackwork to earn money. I'd return home upset, humiliated, and bad-tempered. Lena would ask, "Do you want tea or coffee?"

We hardly talked. There were only brief, businesslike exchanges of information. She said things like "Someone named Beskin called," or "Where is the laundry soap around here?" My literary affairs did not interest her, and I didn't ask her questions, either. Our madness took everyday, commonplace forms.

My routine changed somewhat. Women friends called less and less often. Well, why call if a calm female voice answers the phone?

We remained absolutely unknown to each other.

Lena was unbelievably silent and serene. Hers was not the tense silence of a spoiled loudmouth, and not the menacing silence of an antitank mine, but the silent serenity of a tree root listening absently to the rustle of foliage.

A week went by. Saturday morning I couldn't stand it anymore. I said—no, shouted—"Lena! Listen to me! Let me be completely frank. We are living like a married couple . . . but without the main element of married life. We keep house. You do the laundry. Please, tell me, what does all this mean? I am losing my mind."

Lena looked at me with calm, friendly eyes. "Am I in your way? Do you want me to leave?"

"I don't know what I want! I want to understand. Love I

understand. Lust I understand. I understand everything but this normalized lunacy. If you were a KGB agent, then everything would be normal. I would even be pleased. There would at least be some kind of logic. But this way . . ."

Lena was silent, then said, "If you want me to go, just say so." And then, lowering her narrow Mongolian eyes a little, "If you need *that*—it's all right."

"What do you mean, *that*?"

Her eyelashes lowered even more. Her voice sounded even calmer. "In the sense of physical intimacy."

"No, no," I said. "What for?"

Could I really dare, I thought, destroy this serenity in so gross a way?

About two more weeks passed. And what saved me was vodka. I got drunk at the office party of a progressive publishing house. Made it home around one in the morning. Then— well, how shall I put it best?—I forgot myself. Encroached. Took the wrong road, just like the future jailbird Gurevich.

It was not love, and it was certainly not a "momentary weakness." It was an attempt to ward off chaos.

The stone I threw sank without a ripple to the bottom of the ocean. We didn't even start addressing each other in the familiar form.

A year later, a daughter was born to us, and we named her Katya. That was how we got to know each other.

As a husband, I was a dubious catch. For years I had no steady work. I had the tarnished appearance of a disqualified matador. My stories were not being published. I grew more and more bad tempered, and less and less careful. In the summer of 1970, my first manuscripts found their way to the West.

I began to have foreign acquaintances. They sat in our room till late at night, and gladly drank vodka while they snacked on liver sausage. My communal neighbor Tikhomirov used to mutter in a threatening way, "The people you know! Real Sinyavsky-Daniel types! Troublemakers!"

In the fall of that year, my name was again mentioned on some Western radio stations.

My stories did not interest Lena. In general, she took no interest in accomplishments as such. Her limited outlook seemed a part of her limitless tranquillity.

In this way, my life came under the rule of two opposing elements. An ocean of nonconformism rose to the left. To the right stretched the untroubled calm of bourgeois well-being. And I stumbled along in between.

Meanwhile, Lena had left her job in the beauty parlor and had been hired as a proofreader by Soviet Writer, a publishing house. This surprised me. I didn't know she was so literate. Just as I didn't know a lot of other things, and still don't to this day.

A year later, she entered into conflict with the authorities. Her publishing house had issued a limited edition of Anna Akhmatova's poetry. A very small number of copies were set aside for the staff, but some people were entirely passed over, and included among them was my wife.

She went to see the director of the publishing house, Kondrashev, and stated her claims. In answer, Kondrashev said, "You do not quite grasp the complexity of the political context. The largest part of the edition is being sent abroad. We are obliged to throttle the voice of bourgeois propaganda."

"Throttle mine," Lena told him.

From then on, a partial, fellow-dissident understanding formed between us.

The years went by. Our daughter was growing up. She used to point at my shortwave radio and say, "I put your bee-bee-see on the windowsill."

We had little money; we quarreled often. I would blow up, my wife would be silent. Silence is an enormous power. It ought to be banned by law, like biological warfare.

I was always complaining about not having any future as a writer. Lena would say, "Write two thousand stories. They have to publish *one* of them."

I would think, What's she talking about? What's the use of getting one story published? And I even got offended, though for no reason. We had different senses of scale. I put the emphasis on the unit, Lena on the mass. And she was right. You can only conquer with quantity. All of world history bears this out.

I knew so little about my wife that I was constantly being surprised. Anything that could ruffle her serenity took me by surprise. Once, she burst into tears when someone from the house management committee said something insulting. To be honest, I was even pleased. It meant that her passions could be aroused. But this happened rarely. Most of the time she was imperturbable.

In the 1970s, emigration to the West began. Close friends were leaving. There were endless discussions about whether to leave or not. I kept insisting, "What would there be for me to do there? It makes no sense to run from one's native home! If literature is a reprehensible activity, then our place is in prison."

Lena gave no opinion. She seemed to have become even

more silent. The days dragged on in endless, depressing talk at the dinner table, frequent trips to the airport to see people off, and conversations at night.

I remember well the day in February when Lena came home from work and said, "That's it. We're leaving. I've had it."

I tried to argue. I talked about the motherland, about God, about the benefits of enduring intense social pressure, about the linguistic and cultural range available to us. I even spoke of birch trees—something for which I will never forgive myself. But Lena was already leaving the room to make a telephone call.

I blew up and went off to the Pushkin estate near Pskov for a month. When I returned, Lena handed me a stack of papers to sign for Katya and her. I said, "What, already?"

"Yes," she said, "everything is settled. We have the documents in hand. I'm sure they will let us leave. It could happen within the next two weeks."

I was stunned. I hadn't thought it would happen so soon. More to the point, I had hoped Lena would talk me into leaving with them. After all, it was I who loathed the Soviet regime. Those were *my* stories that weren't being published; it was I who was just a hairsbreadth away from being a dissident.

From then till the day they left, I walked around in a kind of daze. Mechanically did whatever had to be done; greeted guests and saw them off.

The day of departure came at last. A crowd gathered at the airport, mostly my friends and drinking cronies.

We said good-bye. Lena looked completely unperturbed. One of my relatives had given her a silver-fox fur piece as a going-away present. (For a long time afterward, I had dreams of grinning fox faces.) My daughter was wearing big, clumsy sneakers. She looked bewildered. That was the year she wasn't pretty at all.

Then they got on the airplane bus. We waited for the airplane to take off, but planes were taking off every few minutes, and it was hard to tell which one was ours.

I began to miss them on the way back from the airport, and started drinking straight from the bottle in the taxi home. The taxi driver said to me, "At least bend down."

I said, "It doesn't come out well that way."

From that day on, my entire life changed. I was overcome with agitation. The only thing I thought about was emigration. I drank and thought.

Lena wrote postcards that were like coded messages. "Rome is a large beautiful city. By day it's hot. By night they play music. Katya is well. Prices are comparatively low." Her postcards were loaded with calm. My mother read them over and over again, trying to find some shred of emotion. But I knew that was useless.

I will now set down in outline the events that followed:

The accusation of social parasitism and promoting dens of vice. The signed oath not to leave town while under investigation. Investigator Michalev. Some unexplained beatings at a police station. A series of broadcasts on the West German radio. Arrest and trial on Tolmachev Street. Nine days in Kalyaevski Prison. Unexpected release. Summons to the Office of Emigration.

The KGB colonel at the Office of Emigration told me, politely and amiably, "You ought to emigrate. Your wife has left, and you should have left long ago."

Just to be contrary, I said, "My wife and I are divorced. I thought when she left our marriage was all over."

"A divorce would be a mistake. We would like to see your family reunited," the colonel said, smiling broadly. "After all, you love them, don't you?"

"Who is 'them'?"

"Your wife and daughter. Well, of course you love them."

It was in this way that my love for my wife and daughter became a fact. And the person to stand witness to it turned out to be a KGB colonel.

I tried to find my bearings. I could make out two real poles to the world: the known, native, suffocating HERE, and the obscure, half-fantastic THERE. Here, I had a limitless vista of a tormented life among friends and enemies. There, only wife and child, the tiny island of my wife's imperturbable calm.

All my hopes were THERE. I don't know why I gave the colonel a hard time.

Six weeks later, my mother and I were in Austria. Vienna reminded me of a section of Leningrad, the part between the Fontanka and Sadovaya Street. The single serious detail of the city's landscape was the river, the river that I discovered, on the third or fourth day, to be the Danube.

Prostitutes stood out against the grayish backdrop of the streets. They looked like the heroines of foreign-film comedies.

We settled in a little hotel called the Admiral. My mother read Solzhenitsyn day and night. I wrote something or other for émigré journals and newspapers, mostly elaborating on my nonexistent dissident exploits.

By that time, Lena had settled in America. Her letters were more laconic than ever. "I work as a typist. Katya goes to school. Our neighborhood is comparatively safe. Our landlord is a nice, middle-aged American named Andrew Kovalenko."

My mother and I lived in Austria till the summer. Vienna was our stepping stone between Leningrad and America. It's such a long way that it probably has to be done in two hops.

Finally we received our American papers. The seven hours above the ocean seemed like an eternity to me. There is too little in space of any interest. The airplane was already American territory. The airline stewardesses behaved like independent people.

Friends were waiting for us at Kennedy Airport, a well-known photographer named Kulakov, with his wife and son. As soon as the greetings were over, they immediately began railing against life in America.

"Buy a Toyota, old man," Kulakov said, "or, even better, a Volkswagen. American cars are crap!"

I asked, "But where are Lena and Katya?"

Kulakov handed me a note: "Make yourselves at home. We are at the health club. We will be home around eight. There is food in the refrigerator. Lena."

We drove to their apartment in Flushing. The surrounding horizontal landscape reminded me of the wrong side of the Moscow railroad tracks. Skyscrapers were conspicuously absent. My mother looked out the window and said, "The streets are completely empty."

"This isn't a street," Kulakov objected. "This is a highway."

"What does that mean, 'highway'?" my mother asked.

"Main road," I answered.

Lena lived on the first floor of a small brick building.

Kulakov helped carry in our suitcases. Then he said, "Rest up. It's already night in Europe. I'll call you tomorrow." And he left.

I had not expected, of course, to be met by a delegation of American writers. But Lena, I thought, could have come to the airport.

We found ourselves in an empty apartment. There were mattresses on the floor in each of the two rooms. Clothes were strewn all over the place.

Mama took a look in the refrigerator and said, "Cheese here is almost the same as ours."

Suddenly I felt incredible fatigue. I lay down on top of the blanket and lit a cigarette. The contours of reality began to recede.

Who am I, I thought, and where do I come from? What is happening to me? And how will it all turn out? This new life already struck me as too commonplace to hold any significant changes.

I thought, too, how does human intimacy arise? What do people need to have in order to feel kinship?

I woke up early in the morning. Outside the window, a branch was moving back and forth. There was someone beside me. I asked, "Who's there?"

"Lena," answered a calm, female voice, which then said, "You've gotten so heavy! You'll have to start running each morning."

I said, "For all practical purposes, there's no place to run. I'd prefer to stay here. I hope that's possible?"

"Of course. If you love us."

"The colonel says I love you."

"If you love us, then stay. We have no objection."

"What's love got to do with it?" I said. "Love is for teenagers. In our case, it's no longer a matter of love, but of fate. By the way, where's Katya?"

"On a mat, next to her grandmother." Then Lena said, "Look the other way."

I covered my face with an American newspaper. Lena got up, put on a bathrobe, and asked, "Would you like tea or coffee?"

At that moment, Katya appeared. But that's another story.

Katya

Once there was a time when she wasn't here at all, though I can no longer imagine it. Anyway, how can you imagine what wasn't? Then she was brought home, a pink, surprisingly light bundle with lace.

Curious, I remember Katya's childhood much less clearly than my own.

I remember she once got seriously ill, with pneumonia, I think it was. She had to be taken to the hospital. None of us, not even her mother and grandmother, were allowed to visit her. Her condition was critical. We didn't know what to do.

Finally we telephoned the chief physician. He was a generally slovenly person who had usually had too much to drink. He said, "Don't leave your wife and mother alone. Stay by them."

"Meaning what?"

"We will do everything we can," the doctor answered.

"At least let my wife come to the hospital."

"That is forbidden," he said.

Those were terrible days. We sat by the telephone. The black object began to seem like the source of our calamity. The telephone was constantly ringing with calls from light-hearted people who had no idea of what we were going through. My mother would go out onto the landing from time to time to cry.

It happened that an old acquaintance met her there between floors. It was the actor Mercuriev. He and my mother had worked together once. Mother told him about Katya. Mercuriev immediately started digging in his pockets for a two-kopeck piece and went to find a pay phone.

"This is Mercuriev speaking," he said. "Let Norka come to the hospital right away."

And they allowed her to visit at once. Later they also let my wife sit nights with the child. So the only weapon against Soviet administration turned out to be the Absurd.

At any rate, our daughter kept on growing up. She went to kindergarten. Sometimes I would pick her up there. I remember a white wooden bench and a pile of child's clothing, many more things than an adult would ever wear. I recall the stepped-on back of her tiny shoe, and how I used to lift my daughter up by the waist and bounce her gently.

Then we would walk on the street. I can recall the sensation of holding a lively little hand. Even through the mitten you could feel how warm it was.

I was always struck by her helplessness, her vulnerability in the face of public transportation, or the wind . . . her dependence on my decisions, actions, words. . . . I wondered how long this would last, and I would tell myself: until the end.

I once had a conversation with a man I happened to sit next to on a train. He said, "I had always dreamed of having a son, so at first I was bitterly disappointed. Then it was all right. If we had had a boy, I would have given in. I would have reasoned like this: I haven't achieved much myself in life. My son will achieve more. I'll give him the benefit of my failure. He'll grow up to be manly and decisive. So I would have passed into him, as it were, which is to say, I would have ceased to exist. . . . With a daughter it's completely different. She needs me, and that's how it will be to the end of my days. She won't let me forget about myself."

My daughter was growing up. You could already see her when she stood behind an armchair.

I remember she once came home from kindergarten and, without taking off her coat, asked, "Do you love Brezhnev?"

Up to that moment I had never bothered to speak to her about such matters. I had perceived her, I guess, as a kind of precious inanimate object. And now I had to say something, explain.

I said: "You can love people whom you know very well. For example, Mama, Grandma. Or, if worse comes to worst, me. Brezhnev is someone we don't know, though we often see his portrait. Maybe he's a good man. And then, maybe he isn't. How can you love someone you don't know?"

"But our teachers love him," my daughter said.

"Maybe they know him better."

"No," my daughter said, "it's just that they're teachers, and you're only Papa."

From then on she began developing quickly and asking difficult questions. She seemed to have guessed that I was a failure. Sometimes she would ask, "How come they never publish what you write?"

"They don't want to."

"You should write about the dog." My daughter felt I would be brilliant if I wrote about our dog.

So I made up a fairy tale for her. "Once upon a time in a faraway kingdom there lived a man who painted pictures. The king sent for the man and said, 'Paint a picture for me. I will pay you well for it.'

" 'What shall I paint for you?' the painter asked.

" 'Anything you please,' the king answered, 'except for small gray bugs.'

" 'And everything else is all right to paint?' the painter asked, startled.

" 'Well, of course. Everything except for small gray bugs.'

"The painter traveled home. A year went by, then a second and a third. The king began to worry. He commanded his servants to find the painter. When the painter stood before him, the king asked, 'Where is the painting you promised me?'

"The painter hung his head.

" 'Answer,' the king ordered.

" 'I can't paint it,' the painter said.

" 'Why not?'

"There was a long pause. Then the painter said, 'I keep thinking about those small gray bugs.' "

I read this to my daughter and then asked, "Did you understand what I wanted to say?"

"Yes."

130

"What did you understand?"

"He obviously knew them very well."

"Who?"

"The bugs."

Then our daughter started going to school. She did rather well, though she didn't show special gifts for any particular subject. At first this disappointed me. Then I accepted it. After all, talented people have nothing but troubles in life.

Katya's life flowed without any particular upsets. They didn't pick on her at school. I had been much more shy as a child. Then, too, she was supplied with a complete set of parents, and with a grandmother and a dog for good measure.

My daughter treated me very well. A bit of compassion, a bit of contempt. (After all, I couldn't fix an electric appliance. And I didn't bring home very much money either.)

Like all Leningrad schoolchildren, she was precocious. She knew very well what I thought of the authorities. If Brezhnev appeared on television, Katya watched to see what my reaction was.

On the other hand, she would say to me, "Why are you walking around undressed?" It was apparent she found me physically repulsive. Perhaps that's as it should be. That kind of antipathy is common in children (never in parents).

Her character began to turn sour. I gave her a cactus shoot as a present once, and I wrote a little poem to go with it:

> Our little daughter
> Is like this flower;
> She has to prick
> Even those who love her.

In 1978 we emigrated. First my wife and daughter left. Their departure stood for complete and total divorce, though formally my wife and I had gotten divorced some years earlier. Gotten divorced but continued tormenting each other, and there seemed to be no end in sight.

People say that marriages on the brink of divorce are the most stable. But we had gone beyond this point. My wife flew off to America, hoping that the ocean would do what we hadn't managed to accomplish ourselves.

Our daughter left with her. This was natural. And I stayed behind with my mother and Glasha.

I did not want to leave. To be more honest, I knew it was still early. I had to get my manuscripts ready, to exhaust certain possibilities. Or maybe I had to reach the edge, get to the point where madness comes next.

So I stayed behind. My mother remained with me. This, too, was natural.

After my wife and daughter left, events began to move with increasing speed, the way they do in a first novel when an inexperienced writer hurries to write the last pages.

I have now lived in America for four years. My wife and I are together again, though formally we are still divorced. My relationship with my daughter is just as it was before. As before, I lack anything she could possibly admire.

It's not likely I'll become an American rock singer. Or a movie star. Or a drug dealer. It's doubtful I'll ever get rich enough to shield her from material worries.

Besides all that, I still can't drive a car. Nor am I interested in rock music. And the main thing is, I don't speak English well.

Just the other day I heard her say, or rather, speak the following sentence: "So you're finally getting published. So what difference does it make?"

"None at all," I said. "None at all."

Kolya

Before you is the history of our family. I hope it is sufficiently ordinary. There are only a few words left to add.

Last autumn, in mad New York City, my little son was born. He is an American, a citizen of the United States. My wife and I have dubbed him with this unwieldy but accurate title:

"Our own round-the-clock, fully operational, dear little factory of positive emotions."

His name, in Russian, is Nikolai; we call him Kolya. Someday he may be addressed as Mister Nicholas Dowley. He will have his own history, but it will be the history of another, American family.

With Kolya, this book is done. I hope it is clear to everyone that it has been his story.

About the Author

Sergei Dovlatov was born in Ufa, Bashkiria (USSR), in 1941. He dropped out of the University of Leningrad after two years' attendance and was drafted into the army, where he served as a guard in high-security prison camps. In 1965 he began to work as a journalist, first in Leningrad, then in Tallinn, Estonia. After a period of intense harassment by the authorities, he emigrated to the United States in 1978. Mr. Dovlatov, who now lives in Forest Hills, New York, is the author of *The Compromise* and *The Zone*.

About the Translator

Anne Frydman, who translated Mr. Dovlatov's two previous works, teaches literature at The Writing Seminars of The Johns Hopkins University.